SLAP THE GATEKEEPER

SLAP THE GATEKEEPER

Correcting the inner voice
that only allows the bad in
and will only let the good out

DOUGLAS HODGES

Douglas Hodges

This work has two audiences in mind. The first audience is those who are on a journey towards mental health and are looking for practical help. I hope you will find that here as we talk through how mental illness grows and develops, and how to make changes in your present to have a better life.

The second audience is those who have a friend or loved one who is experiencing mental illness, and you are just trying to better understand your friend. If this is you, and you are here for a friend, welcome. You may be an invaluable resource for your loved one or friend as they navigate this journey.

From the bottom of my heart, whether you are here for you or for somebody else, thank you for being here. I hope you find what follows as appropriately challenging and encouraging.

Contents

Chapter 1

Introduction

Does it ever seem like other people just don't have problems? Or you think that you are the only one who has to struggle? Have you ever wondered why you are able to do all kinds of good for other people but can't let anybody do anything good for you? How about when bad things naturally find a home in your head. These include the comments that others merely made but really get stuck in your head? Maybe it's the words of a bully from elementary school or the damning judgement of an abusive parent? Or it could it be the breakup speech you heard from your first crush? Wherever or however it was birthed, it grew up inside your head and seemed to have no way of leaving. It is almost like there is a door in your head that is locked from the outside and controlled by a gatekeeper. It seems as though the gatekeeper is operating outside your control and gets to determine what is allowed to enter and what is allowed to go out. Even though you talk nicely to the gatekeeper, the gatekeeper has made no indication of changing course.

If this is you, you have a jacked-up gatekeeper. And by gatekeeper, I mean that imaginary person who lives in your brain that tells you what thoughts can come out and what thoughts can go in. When he (I just went ahead and made him a he, but if it helps you to make him a her or an it, feel free) gets jacked-up, he tends to operate the gates of good and bad in your mind consistently backwards, such that he allows good things out, but does not let good things in, or he allows bad things in but does not let bad things out. You can encourage others, instruct others, be there for others, but because he is jacked up, he never lets any of that helpful stuff come your way. The only thing that is allowed into your mind is the bad. Even if what is coming to your gate is really good, somehow he messes with it and turns it into bad.

To make matters worse, he won't let you get rid of any of the bad. He forces you to keep it all bottled up inside and will not allow you to let any of it out. It is better to think of yourself as bad and be the only one than to talk about it and have others agree with you. After all, clearly, you are bad through and through, and if you ever let down your guard and let the bad out, others will see you for who you really are. So you see, the gatekeeper is doing you a favor by only letting the good out, because we would not want everybody to know how bad you really are, right?

Think of it like this; If your brain were a restaurant and your gatekeeper was the cook, people could come and visit, and you could serve them really good food. But when it was time to prepare a meal yourself, your gatekeeper made you dig around in the trash and eat the rotten scraps your guests left, and he only lets you eat alone.

Do you see how messed up the gatekeeper is? Sometimes he just needs to be slapped. Sometimes you wish he would go on a vacation, even for a weekend, and let you live a life free from his tyrannical control. But if he does and leaves you in charge of the gate, even for just a bit, it freaks you out! You have never let the good in before; where would you even put it if you allowed it in? There is no place for it. So out of fear, you just keep with the tradition. Even when you are in control of your thoughts, it is still him controlling you. You just can't break free.

Would you like to know how to better control that gatekeeper and be in a better position to take charge of yourself(what goes out and what comes into your mind)? Then keep reading. We will first take a journey into the origins of the gatekeeper and figure out how he came to be the way he is. From there, we will empower you with some pretty cool strategies to slap the gatekeeper right up beside his head to bring him into submission. Finally, we will wrap up with a few strategies to keep your gatekeeper in line and follow the straight and narrow.

If what you just read describes a loved one in your life, and you just don't understand how or why they are the way they are, then keep reading this book. While this will not describe any specific person's story, it might give you a little empathy as to how and why they think and act the way they do. This will not give you a direct remedy, but if you are not directly impacted by a messed up gatekeeper, it might help you be a better friend. As a mental health counselor, the one thing I repeatedly hear from my patients is how they wish they had a friend who could understand and be there for them. So, if this is you, kudos to you.

PART 1

How the Bad Gatekeeper Forms

Your gatekeeper was not always like this. He has a back story. He was formed and molded to be the way he his. It is highly likely that he formed the way he did for a good reason, likely to protect you from something that was to overwhelming to deal with otherwise. However, this is not suggesting that we should leave him alone(that's the bad gatekeeper talking), instead, it is wise to take a trip into his past to see how he formed. Once we can understand how he was formed, then we can better prepare to slap him into line. What was once formed as protection for you might now be your prison!

Chapter 2

Seminal Event

Somewhere in your past, something happened; let's just call this a *Seminal Event*. No, we are not talking about semen; we are looking at the other definition of that word. A seminal event is something that happens that greatly influences your future or alters your understanding of reality. For example, it may be a movie you saw that totally inspired you (for me, it was Top Gun, I forever felt the need for speed), maybe it was your first taste of a certain food or your first exposure to a sport. These are all positive and fun seminal events. Also, these can be great influencers of gatekeepers; the teacher that tells you how smart you are, the coach that tells you what a great athlete you are, the parent who beats you unconscious while telling you how you ruined their life and how they wished you had never been born.

Oh, sorry, we went dark really quick there. I guess I should have eased into that one, but that is not typically how the seminal events that form bad gatekeepers work. You don't get a warning. It's not like you get an invitation that in two weeks that person who is supposed to love and protect you is gonna start molesting you, so get ready. Or that an accident will happen next Tuesday and take away your mom. You don't really get a warning. It just comes out of the blue. You are minding your own business, going about life as usual, following what you know to be the rules as best as you know, and bam, it just happens. And it can't unhappen. You can't ever go back. At that moment, whatever your seminal event is (not was, because you are still likely experiencing it), actually changed your world. Life will never be the same again.

This event informed you that you are not like everybody else. Because of this event, you don't deserve what everybody else has. You just don't measure up and you have the scar to prove it. You see that scar; you feel that scar, or maybe the only way you are even alive is because of that scar. Whatever caused it, however it came to be, it will never go away. How do you know? You have tried. You have tried everything you know to make it go away, but it didn't go. Maybe it is a string of relationships that you invited in to remove the scar, or it was a substance you used to try to wipe it off. Perhaps it is covered up on the outside with a tattoo or a bunch of religion, or you have been to a thousand different therapists, but nobody is ever allowed into that main event. Some get close, some even knock on the door, but you kick those people out of your life QUICK! Nobody is allowed to see that. In fact, you are about two sentences away from tossing this book aside and leaving a negative review about how stupid it is if I keep talking about your seminal event.

I do not want to sound insensitive here. You may need to take a break, but please don't stop this journey. In this book, my goal is not to create further pain but to help you identify the roots of this messed-up gatekeeper and help you change things for good. I am sorry that this event happened to you. In case nobody has ever said it to you, you did not deserve it.

I can imagine that you don't want to think about it. You did not want it to happen, and you don't want to remember it. But the main problem is that you can't forget it. It is always there. It influences you every day. It has affected how you view the world because it left you with a jacked-up gatekeeper who keeps reinforcing the narrative of what you perceived the seminal event to be.

From that moment, the gatekeeper who had previously been able to let in both the good and bad just stopped letting the good in. Whatever it was that happened to you changed that gatekeeper. While it might be tempting to think that this was just a bad reaction to a really bad event, I want to invite you to think differently about it. Yes, something really bad happened to you, but what if changing what the gatekeeper allows in and out was your best available option? I know it sounds like I am talking out of both sides here, but hang with me for a moment.

When that event happened, you encountered a tremendous amount of pain. The pain could have been physical, but more than likely, it was psychological or spiritual pain. Maybe it was all three. But the psychological and spiritual pain is the major type of pain that I want to focus on for a minute because it is the more intense pain. This pain doesn't heal easily; the pain that painkillers can't touch. When you encounter that type of pain, you would want to do all you can to make sure that you never reencounter it. When your seminal event happens, your logic is not so great. Partly because you are in pain and potentially because you were really young when this happened, and your brain was not fully developed. You were dealing with adult-level pain in a child-level brain. And you really don't want that to ever happen again.

So one major concession that you make is that you give up. When you give up, you protect yourself from hurt. When you stop hoping to be treated fairly and you learn to expect abuse, undoubtedly, it will still hurt physically, but giving up is the price you pay to no longer be hurt psychologically or spiritually. Your brain simply learns to agree with the assumption that your seminal event is leading you to conclude, and from this point onward, it only allows the bad in. By only allowing bad in, in all sincerity, your gatekeeper believes he is doing you a favor. By leading you to assume that you are a bad person, you don't have to worry about ever having to be blindsided by an unworthy feeling. You just have to learn how to agree with the premise and move on with life. If somebody ever tries to make a positive deposit into you, that might feed or fuel a different type of hope-filled thinking. In that case, your gatekeeper learns that this is just going to open the door to hurt and pain, so he quickly dismisses the idea. Why? Because it is better to limp through life with a deformed foot than to die from a potential amputation.

To be factual, hope has probably not worked out greatly for you. Every time you hope for something or in someone, it or they have likely not come through. In all reality, it may not have been every time. But every time it happens, your gatekeeper definitely keeps a record of it. In rare times when you hoped and what you hoped for actually happened, your gatekeeper saw that as a fluke and quickly dismissed it as such (we will talk more about this later). So, to keep you from catastrophic losses, as you experienced with your first seminal event, the gatekeeper has just taken over and only allowed the bad to come into your mind.

If any of the above sounds familiar to you, please don't give up. There is a path to a better life. It is a defined path, and I have seen countless people go through it. Though it is not an easy path, there is a path. The easy paths lead to many disappointments because they don't work, at least not consistently in the long run. As we keep going, make sure you take breaks and take time to breathe. If you find your muscles getting tight as you read or your jaw is clench-ing, take a few seconds to relax them. Make sure you get some water too. (More on this to come)

Chapter 3

Lose Your Voice

So your Seminal event has happened, and you are in recovery mode. When you are feeling hurt from the pain, and you are trying to heal or you are evaluating your options, and something swells up inside of you; the part of you that still has hope, and says, "HEY, this is not right, I can't be treated like this!" Then you make a plan to go tell somebody about how poorly you have been or are being treated. Maybe you confront your accuser or go to a person you assumed to be safe, and you gain the courage to tell them how bad it is for you. And in response to your hope-filled actions... they just take your voice.

"Mom, dad has been asking me to do things that make me feel uncomfortable." — *"Oh honey, he is your father and he loves you. You just need to do what he says."*

"I am really sad after the accident, I wish mom were still here." — *"You are not the only one suffering here. Maybe you can just keep thoughts like that to yourself."*

"My boyfriend is really not treating me well." — *"I don't want to hear it. We all told you he was bad , now you have made your bed and you need to lie in it."*

"Pastor, I don't think God could love me after what I did." — *"That's nonsense; God loves everybody. Stop being so dramatic."*

Sometimes, the people who take your voice don't even realize they have taken your voice. They likely did not recognize the gravity of the situation you were facing, and you likely did not have the language skills to communicate how intense the pain of the situation was/is. Because you were young, they attempted to just placate you and help you move on to the next thing. But unfortunately, there was no moving on from this. And you really need(ed) help. {*For those reading this in a position to help someone, when somebody comes to you and asks for help, take a moment to listen. Especially if they are a little kid. You may be the only person in their life who can listen and hear! What they are saying may not be what they are meaning. Take a few moments to ask a question and listen. This can be the difference between bondage and freedom for somebody.*}

Other times, the person you were reaching out to for help may not have had a voice themselves. They may have been in such pain when they were facing their own issues and did not have a way of dealing with them. Telling you to just remain silent, or encouraging you to just move on may have been how they learned to deal with their own pain. Unfortunately for both of you, those ways can be really unhealthy.

Sometimes, the person who takes your voice is also the person who is causing your pain. Often, abusers will tell their victims that if they tell anybody what has happened, things will just worsen. This could be a threat to your life or to the lives of your friends and family. And other times, you are led to believe that you will be responsible for any harm that comes to your abuser if you tell somebody.

Whether the person who took your voice did so unintentionally, passively or if they did so out of evil intentions, the end result was the same. You lost your voice. But why is this so important? How does this influence that negative gatekeeper in your head? How is this still influencing you still today?

Losing your voice is to lose a part of what makes you human. It is really losing part of who you are. Let's zoom out from you for a minute and talk for a bit about something that is not you. (I know you really needed this break!) When a political dictator takes over a country, one of the first things they do is to restrict the press. When they have the power to stop people from speaking against them and can control the "voice" of their opposition, they can pretty much get away with whatever they like. But controlling the narrative is not just for evil dictators. Politicians who are successful in getting elected where there is a free press are successful in staying on message and allowing one voice out of their campaign. Therefore, everybody who speaks for, about, or even to the candidate is using the same voice. Whoever can accomplish this is likely the person who will win the election. Controlling the news cycle is the job of every press secretary, and learning how to take the most horrific news about your boss and "spin" it to something that is on message, keeps your boss in power and keeps you employed.

Your outer voice is the first step to being able to control your inner voice. If I can control what you say, after a while,

I can control what you think. The inverse is also true. If I can control what you think, I can control what you say. If you think this is a bunch of hogwash, do a little research on how much money is spent on advertisements each year. When you go to a store, take a moment to think about what is influencing you to go to the store you just went to. What is influencing you to select the product you just placed in your cart, and what motivates you to use the specific form of payment you just used to buy it? Companies invest a large sum of money into advertisements because they want you to have their voice (about their product). Simple slogans or catchy jingles fill your mind subconsciously when you decide how to use your hard-earned money.

You may be wondering why the lesson on political science and advertising, so here is the connection. How you internalize the world around you significantly influences your actions. When someone takes away your ability to get help processing something you were never designed to process alone, you are left at a disadvantage. It is almost like trying to put together a piece of furniture from Ikea® without the screwdriver. Sure, you have all that parts and all the fasteners, but it will never go together correctly and securely without the one tool needed to make it all work!

When you make a point to speak out about the injustice that has happened or is happening to you, and the people you go to for support either won't listen or refuse to believe you, it is another pain that encourages your gatekeeper to keep the bad in. The seminal event keeps the good out, and losing your voice reinforces that you should keep the bad in. NOBODY CARES what you are going through. And since nobody cares, you should just suck it up and learn to deal with it yourself because you are the only one you can count on. Nobody else wants to hear what you have to say, and nobody else wants to help you. After a while, you will realize that it isn't that people are not willing to help you, but they are not just able to help. After all, if they were able and willing to help, they would have done so the first time you talked about it. If talking helps so much, why am I being prescribed all of these meds? If talking about things is so helpful, why do so many relationships end so poorly after you open up just a little about the hurt you live with? If talking helps, why is it so freaking painful to do it!?

Losing your voice after a major pain keeps you trapped. And to protect you from future pain, just like with the seminal event, the gatekeeper tells you it is best to stop trying to let the bad out. In order to protect yourself, it is better just to keep all of that bad inside because the pain of being rejected is so great. So, it is better to just deal with it yourself. After all, you are starting to internalize that you are a bad person, so you might as well own it. Soon, it becomes less about 'change', and more about adjusting to a new normal. You view yourself as an amputee adjusting to a new prosthetic limb. No amount of talking is going to make your leg grow back, so you might as well just suck it up, buttercup and learn to walk with a limp and accept certain activities that are no longer available to you. Things like fulfilling relationships, a life filled with joy, good health, and exciting futures are for people who have all of their extremities and not for you.

Losing your voice does not mean that you lose the argument(about wanting good) with yourself, rather, it means there is no other person to argue with. Nothing pushes back. Nothing challenges the gatekeeper at this point. Any attempt to challenge the gatekeeper is dismissed immediately as inapplicable to you. It's like a boarding announcement at the airport for a plane that might be leaving from your same gate, but it's not your flight. No sense even paying attention to it. It's just going to waste your time and get you more frustrated. Just go back to your phone and play your game; you are stuck here.

PART 2

How the Gatekeeper Grows

Your seminal event and losing your voice give birth to the messed-up gatekeeper in your head. Without those two events, you likely don't get a negative gatekeeper. Some have a seminal event, and when they tell their loved ones about it, they hear them and help formulate a healthy plan for the pain to stop and for a possible path to recovery. If this happens, the gatekeeper never goes negative. He is still there in your mind, but he learns not to let the bad in. And that it is ok and healthy to let bad out if any bad temporarily does find its way in.

But when the seminal event happens and you lose your voice, there are a few other elements that typically co-occur and tend to grow the power of the gatekeeper. These items tend to reinforce the negative thinking and continue to give him strength and allow him to expand his reach into your thoughts.

Chapter 4

Pleasing Others

Your seminal event teaches you that you are a bad person, so there is no point in accepting anything good. Losing your voice tells you that life will be a lot smoother if you just deal with it and stop talking about it, and that makes you keep the bad in. While you have concluded that this must be true for you, you really don't like it. And since you can't change any of this for yourself, perhaps you can change it for others. So, you make it your life's mission to please others!

So you might be tempted to think, "Come on now, pleasing others is a good thing. How are you going to make it out to be something that is evil?! You are starting to sound like those people who stole my voice! Don't take this away from me!"

Don't get me wrong; doing good for others is not necessarily bad. Helping a friend or even a stranger in need is a healthy and loving thing. And even though your gatekeeper might not be able to fully allow you to internalize it, helping somebody in need still feels good. But this is not what I am talking about. Pleasing others, as it relates to messed up gatekeepers, is less about helping those in need and more about finding yourself trapped in helping to enable those who are all too quick to take advantage of you.

When in the course of helping someone they do something you don't like or something that is painful for you, and you cannot speak up for yourself to tell them to stop, this leads you to feeling trapped...again! You help somebody, you see how good it makes them feel, and while you get a little bit of a contact buzz from their happiness, low and behold, they need your help again. And again, and again! Pretty soon, because you just don't ever say no, these "takers" just keep coming and to ask from you. Initially, it started as a really good thing, but now it is driving you crazy. Can't they see how rude or destructive they are? The sad part is that they really can't. Your gatekeeper's perverted cousin lives inside their head. They learned to only let out the bad and only let in the good.

Now, let's get back to you. Pleasing others at this level typically starts when you are young. After your seminal event and after you lose your voice, the trouble and dysfunction did not stop there. It was still causing a great deal of chaos in your life. So you picked up a tool to bring some sort of order to the chaos. Pleasing others was that tool. If you could just make dad laugh, maybe he would not beat mom tonight. If you did all of the laundry, washed all the dishes and made dinner, maybe mom would not get drunk tonight. If you were the first to do all of your homework and volunteered to stay after school and help the teacher, maybe she would praise you, and you could receive the only healthy praise that was not connected to an abusive act.

Maybe pleasing others was your only ticket out of the chaos. Perhaps good grades gave you a chance to leave. Perhaps being the first in and the last out at your sport gave you a fighting chance for a scholarship. Maybe it involved a religious youth group where you never really felt worthy enough to belong, so you thought you needed to work harder and be nicer than others to deserve your place at the table.

Whatever your reasons, all of this served as a vitamin supplement for your gatekeeper. His tyrannical rule of your thoughts and behaviors just increased. The more you please others, at the expense of your own personal growth, the more entrenched your gatekeeper gets. As long as you can continue to let the good out and keep the bad securely locked inside, you have peace, a place, and a purpose. Talk to somebody about what is really going on at home and why you don't want to go there? That's just plain crazy talk! If these people knew who you really were, they would kick you to the curb and it would feel just like how it felt at the seminal event. We don't want that again, now do we? So you plug along. You rock and roll with pleasing others. And the more you do it, the better you get at telling people what they want to hear. Also, the easier it gets to deceive yourself that you really like it and that others deserve happiness and you don't. Did you catch that? Your gatekeeper is growing and gaining strength.

Every so often, the pleaser in you just gets fed up. You give and give and give, and finally, you just blow up at a point of desperation. You can't take it anymore, and you emotionally vomit all over somebody. You take a good 10-15 seconds and just tell them off. You tell them what a jerk they are, and how much they take from you without ever giving anything in return. And while speaking, the words were really flowing out of your mouth like butter on a roll right out of the oven. In the middle of it, you find yourself being a little proud that you could audibly put together this string of hurtful insults. You did not know you had it in you. For a minute, you think, this must be what it feels like to plant a flag on top of Mount Everest. It is almost a dissociative experience, meaning its like you are outside of you watching you do this, and you are like, "Yea me!".

During your emotional vomit, it was like you were in a boxing match with your gatekeeper, and you have him on the ropes. You are landing some serious blows and starting to get a rhythm. For a brief moment, you think, "maybe today is the day I knock this jerk out." But your gatekeeper is a wise old fighter. For a few seconds, he defends himself while you tire yourself out, and then, just when you start to have hope, out of nowhere, he counterpunches.

At this point, you realize the quiver in the lip of the recipient of your tirade. You see the tears form in their eye as they begin to process what a tool they are, and all of that joy you experienced 3 seconds ago turns into a giant pile of poo. Left hook, right jab, body punch, body punch, right hook to the chin, and out of nowhere, a guy is standing over you saying, "Six, seven, eight..."

You stood up for yourself because you could not take it anymore, but your gatekeeper has used this entire experience to just add strength to himself. Once again, you let out some bad, and the one thing you were good at, which is pleasing others, was taken away from you. Did you see how bad you made that person feel? You know they have problems, and they can't help but be like they are. You, of all people, should recognize that. How dare you add to their pain. Don't you have enough pain of your own to deal with? This is exactly why we don't let any of that out. You should probably plan to move out of state. Make sure that you never see that person again. Go ahead and give them all the money you have on you and offer to pay for their therapy. You and you alone are solely responsible for their unhappiness.

Even in defeat, the gatekeeper, like a politician taking advantage of a natural disaster, figures out a way to gain power and beat you down. So while pleasing others may look like a good thing, when your gatekeeper desperately needs slapping, pleasing others just becomes a way to keep the gatekeeper strong. When you get a chance to slap your gatekeeper, then you can please others and yourself without harming yourself. You are able to make decisions out of love and freedom; not out of guilt or obligation. More to come on this in part 2. But before we get there, let us look at a few other things that happen to fortify your gatekeeper's stronghold.

Chapter 5

Good = Waiting for the Next Bad Thing

Despite the seminal event that now only allows bad in, the losing of the voice that keeps you from letting any of the bad out, and the strengthening that happens to the gatekeeper when you are taken advantage of, despite all of this, every once in a while, a little piece of good sneaks past the gatekeeper. It is almost like the gatekeeper turns around in desperation and says, "Shoot, how did you make it through?".

Here are some examples. Maybe it is a compliment from somebody you really respect or a gift from an unexpected source. It could be a thank you card from somebody you know has no way of having ulterior motives. You start to think for a minute that this gesture of kindness might actually be true. You did not do anything to get this good. It is not repayment for something you did. It is not trans-actional. Sometimes this unexpected good is not personal. Maybe it is a bonus at work, an unexpected refund on your taxes, a break that just simply comes your way. Something fortunate happened to you. There is no way to deny it; no way to ignore it. A really good thing just happened.

But here's the problem, you have absolutely nowhere to put something good. Because you have never really thought about the good coming your way, much less actually *having* good come your way, so there is no place to put it. It's almost like somebody just gave you a $100,000 9 ft. Steinway Piano, but you live in a studio apartment. It is really valuable and beautiful, but not only do you have nowhere to put it, but you also don't know how to play the piano! Neverthelesss, you like it, so much that you are willing to take piano lessons.

If you receive this good, you might have to rearrange a little bit of this bad in the corner. You may even need to get rid of some of it. A part of you wants to receive this good and plant it so that it might grow into a little bit of hope! But the gatekeeper knows better. The gatekeeper was there the last time something good came along. He remembers when that cute guy who eventually became your boyfriend told you that you were beautiful and that he loved you, and then he reminds you how devastated you were when you got dumped at the Waffle House at 2:00 AM! He then reminds you of that job you moved to take because your friend was the boss and promised it would be different. Also, he reminds you of how lonely you felt when you worked yourself into a nervous breakdown and your friend was nowhere to be found.

Really, I don't think your gatekeeper is intentionally trying to be a jerk. He came to be for a reason. Most of the time, he has come to be because he is desperately trying to keep you from getting hurt. He was there to pick up the pieces when all of these tragedies came your way. He was the only one around trying to help you make sense of it all. Unfortunately, he also prevented you from hearing or receiving any other voices. However, listening to others got you hurt in the first place, so you just learn to listen to him and him alone. Not because he is always right, but because he is always there. You don't like what he has to say, you may not even agree with it, but he is very consistent.

So when good comes your way, somehow, when it magically makes it through despite his best efforts, the gatekeeper quickly gobbles it up and tells you that anything good that happens to you is just a reminder that something bad is coming. And because you lost your voice a long time ago, there is no argument.

As much as you want to receive the good and allow it to grow, there are just too many experiences in your past where you have previously received good, placed too much hope in them and got burned...hope. There was a time when you had hope and that hope always led to disappointment. That new baby was supposed to fix the relationship. That new car was supposed to make you happy. He promised he would love you forever if you would just send him that picture... and we know how that turned out.

Over and over again, good has just been a reminder that while it is a nice thought, long-term good is for other people. It is like playing roulette. The promise of a 35 to 1 return looks really great, but that little ball never lands on your number. And when it does, you better cash out and head home to find a place to bury it because it might never happen again. For you, experiencing something good is just a painful reminder of all other good things that never panned out and eventually ended up in hurt and pain. Now, it is your gatekeeper's job to help you remember that and deal with it. Good is just another gamble, and the house always wins. It is better to just stay miserable and be consistent than to risk the hurt and pain of chasing after the good. It is a fool's errand. It is a waste of time and resources.

Chapter 6

Culture/Gender Roles

The seminal event lets the bad in; losing your voice keeps the bad in. Pleasing others and getting used strengthens the gatekeeper, and any attempt to receive good is a reminder that bad is just going to eventually come. But at this point, a few elements tend to add a layer of complexity to the situation. These are culture and gender roles. Sometimes, these two separate and distinct issues compound. Let's see if either of these or both apply to you.

In some cultures, there is just an expectation that bad will always come your way. Bad was never a house guest; bad was the landlord for as long as anybody can remember. Good never happened to you, and good did not happen to anybody you knew. Nobody in your family and nobody in your extended family ever made it. Well, there was that one guy, but you don't really claim him. He pretty much had to forsake all that the family held dear. So we can't really count him, even though he had a pretty good life. But others have tried to replicate his success and failed miserably, so he was just the exception.

And maybe it is not just your family, perhaps it is your entire county or your entire country! Everybody's life just plain sucks. How could you ever hope for anything but bad to ever come your way? It has never come to anybody. You go to church and sing about how bad it is. You go to the Olympic Games and bet on how much your country will lose. Losing becomes your mission. You are honored for having lost the most.

Another issue is gender. Maybe you had the misfortune of being born a certain gender, and in your culture, your gender makes it impossible to enjoy life. Maybe your gender is doomed to be dominated by the other gender. Maybe your gender is assumed to always be strong and never have needs. Maybe your gender is not allowed to have needs. Or your gender is not allowed to ever help meet needs. Your culture and gender add a layer of complexity to your gatekeeper problem. I have learned that just because you think you got the short end of the culture or gender stick, it does not mean that the grass is always green on the other side. It could be better, which is what your gatekeeper tells you, but in all reality, it is just different. But this is the key; it does not really matter whether your culture is great or your gender is divine. What matters is what your gatekeeper tells you about your culture or your gender. People like us don't ask for help. People of our gender don't get to have opinions. People who live where we live never make it.

Your gatekeeper forms an opinion about your culture, and it may or may not be accurate. The accuracy of the opinion is not really the point, but the degree to which you are convinced is important. The more you are convinced that your struggles with your culture and your gender are true, the more your gatekeeper will use it to strengthen his position.

Here are a few possible examples of this...

> *So just because you go to school and get a fancy education, it doesn't make you better than the rest of us. You will just return here with a whole bunch of debt, and work at the same plant with the rest of us.*

> *You think because you make money now, you don't have to help your brother? You know that you are the only one who can help him. No matter how much money you make, he will always be your brother.*

> *Young ladies don't talk like that. Don't ever let me hear those words coming out of your mouth again.*

> *Man up!*

> *Woman up!*

> *Just be good to the gentlemen Fancy, and they'll be good to you!*

Your gatekeeper speaks the language of your gender and your culture. It's the only language that he knows. If you are reading this in English, you are likely thinking in English. Even if I wrote this in Spanish, and let's say you learned Spanish, you are going to translate it back to English so you can internalize it. When you have had a seminal event and have lost your voice, your gatekeeper tends to take the worst parts of whatever culture or whatever gender you have experienced, and it convinces you that you are the net sum of all that is bad. Those early negative experiences have cemented the reality that you are bad, other people are good, and there is no hope of changing it. You will always be like you are, and everybody else around you is just the same. People that made it out of the culture or achieved beyond what your culture allowed for your gender were just weird freaks and not worthy of being compared to you. You are just like everybody else.

Chapter 7

Hyper Independence

All of this sums to lead you to a state of hyper independence. People don't add anything to your life; they just take from you. Besides, people don't really want you either. Good people want other good people. And the ones who want you don't know the real you. If they did, they would have you arrested or something.

So the further you get in life, the more it is necessary to be able to depend on yourself. You are the only one who knows you. You are the only one who will put up with you. You are the only one who can understand you. The sooner you can come to grips with the fact that nobody likes you, nobody is like you, and you are just going to be like you are forever, the sooner you can figure out how to simply function in life.

At this point in your life, your gatekeeper is strong. You are not only drinking his Koolaid; you are manufacturing it and wearing the t-shirt. You are so entrenched in his teachings that you have become his disciple and evangelist. You are preaching the bad news of misery and destruction to all who will hear it. The more you share the horrible truth that people suck, and the less people want to be around you. And thus, you have also now become his prophet.

The only other people you might even hope to partner with are people who are just like you. They have been hurt, jacked up, and don't deserve good, but they do like pleasing others. So you go to church, you sing in the choir, people tell you what a great job you do, and you go home and get drunk and pass out on the couch because you just can't handle it. You go to the gym, pump your iron, and people tell you how ripped you are, but you come home and purge all the food you just ate. You may have found a spouse, but your relationship sucks. You don't talk with each other, and you don't have sex. You don't share dreams. You just pay bills together and transport children from place to place. There's no point in working on the marriage because people like you don't have good marriages, and besides, who else is going to put up with you.

So, you find ways to meet whatever needs you to have by yourself. Maybe those needs are met with pornography, with chemicals, with an online shopping cart, or you pretend to be somebody else from time to time and hit the clubs to flirt or to hook up. Perhaps you go on elaborate vacations to scratch your itch, to remind yourself of a life you will never live. Either way, independence is your one virtue. The less you depend on other people, the more complete of a person you become. And one day, you will ultimately achieve your goal. You will die miserable and alone and have instructions to have you cremated (because you can't find 6 friends to be pallbearers) and just have your ashes flushed down the toilet. Now that's a life well-lived. Nobody cries, nobody cares. You have been able to completely isolate and insulate yourself from the rest of the world. You are entirely independent. Nobody was ever able to hurt you again; you took care of that all by yourself!

BUT...there is another way.

PART 3

Slapping the Gatekeeper

So, how far did you get in part one before you skipped here? I know, some of it may have been a little bit intense. Or, maybe some of it did not fully apply to you. Or, perhaps you just did not care so much about figuring out how your gatekeeper came to be; you just want him gone. However, you made it to part two. Welcome! I hope the investment of time you take reading these next few sections will be an investment into a new way of processing the world. Ultimately, I hope you will be able to slap your gatekeeper. Going down this journey will help you learn to let the bad out, let the good in, find your voice, and learn how to evaluate the type of people you help so that the people you help have a chance to also invest in you. When you slap your gatekeeper into a better way of living and learn how to keep slapping him (because it will take more than one slap), you will be able to confront parts of your culture that are unhealthy, and challenge inappropriate gender stereotypes and become the healthiest version of yourself.

Are you a little scared? Maybe you heard this all before, and maybe you even sent in the $24.95 for the magic prayer towel to make all of this happen. Or it sounds like a little pie in the sky for you. My guess is that your gatekeeper is really acting out right now, telling you that you should probably put this down. Making you believe that this is for other people.

What you will encounter in this next section has the potential to change your life; It will not change your past. Nobody can do that. It will not magically make it all better, but you have the chance to change your present and ultimately change your future. But in doing this, there is a high likelihood that you will encounter some emotions that are new and fresh, or emotions that are old and strong. As you do this, it is my desire that you work with these emotions healthily and safely.

Let me give you some broad guidelines to consider when responding to emotions. Much like the white lines that surround a sports field, I want to tell you what is out of bounds. There are a wide range of responses that can healthily take place in bounds, and you will likely need the whole field to progress to health. But, here are the lines around the field.

First, anything that is harmful to you is out of bounds. Anything that would injure you is unhealthy. This starts with cutting or intentionally inflicting physical pain on yourself, and it also includes any attempt to take your life. If you start having these thoughts, reach out for help; don't have those thoughts alone. . Call a hotline, and talk to a professional (more on this shortly). At the very least, allow yourself a 24-hour period before acting on any of these plans. Make talking to somebody a part of that 24-hour plan.

A second boundary is anything you take or engage in that is designed or intended to quickly numb the pain. This could be a chemical you ingest, the money you recklessly spend, or unhealthy sexual acts. While it is true that these actions will numb your pain, they will not solve it. In fact, these acts will just add to your pain and increase the time and effort it takes to get healthy.

The third line in this field is any desire to hurt others. As you work through your past and uncover some intense things, you may have a desire to physically or psychologically harm those who harmed you in retaliation. While you may have a great reason to do so, this will not solve your problem. It is better and healthier if you go through the proper authority.

This leads to the fourth boundary, which is isolation. Do not go through this alone. If you have a close friend you can trust, now is the time to lean on them. If you don't have a close friend you can trust, hire one. This is where you need a good counselor. There are many options for finding a counselor, and it is easy to get lost in an alphabet of letters that follow the names of counselors. But what do they all mean? Where do you go to find someone who can help you get through whatever difficult situation you are facing? Here are a few pointers.

1. Know What Type of Professional You Need
   There is a big difference between a psychiatrist, a psychologist, and a counselor. While there are some overlaps, here are some basic guidelines.
   You can only get medicine from a medical doctor. A

psychiatrist is a medical doctor. They will typically manage medications. While some psychiatrists will talk to you, it is very unusual for this profession to spend time helping you work through your thoughts and emotions. They will typically refer you to a counselor or a psychologist.

A psychologist has a doctoral degree, but still not a medical doctor. Typically, a psychologist will specialize in administering psychological tests and can be very helpful in determining an exact diagnosis. Some will also provide counseling services, but most will not.

A counselor or psychotherapist will help you work through your thoughts or behaviors to achieve emotional, relational and spiritual health. A good counselor will work with your doctors and heed the diagnostic material provided by a psychologist, should you have one.

If you are able to find a practice that has all three, it is awesome. That way, they can work as a team to help you from different angles to get better.

2. Look for State Licensure

A counselor who the state has licensed has met a certain set of professional credentials. In addition to setting a standard, the state licensure boards also manage complaints filed for a counselor. This is important because if a person is not licensed, there is no way or platform to know their history. Counselors are trained and licensed as social workers, mental health counselors, licensed professional counselors, marriage and family counselors, or addiction counselors.

People often try to pass along "certifications" as the

same or similar to being licensed, but these are two entirely different things. Some licensed counselors have particular certifications in certain therapeutic practices, but there are also agencies who will issue a certificate for the right price. If your counselor does not have a state license, and only a purchased certification, if there is ever a complaint or concern about them, the unscrupulous counselor will simply go find another body to certify them, and you will never know about it.

Check out your state's licensure website to verify that a person has a license, and that it is clear and active.

3. Ask for References From People You Trust

Check with your doctor, pastor, or other community leaders. If you have friends who have used the services of professional counselors, ask them who they might recommend. If you are looking to use your insurance, you will likely need to call your insurance company and ask for a list of providers who will accept your insurance. Then, take that list to your doctor, pastor, or trusted friend to help you narrow it down. Some counselors will have bios on their website, which can help you decide. Even if you don't have a pastor you could trust, or you don't want your pastor or doctor to know, call a few churches or community centers (as they are likely referring people to counselors on a regular basis), and see whose name keeps popping up on the list.

4. You Can't Always Trust Websites

Not every good counselor is gifted in web design. And not every person who is gifted in web design is a good counselor. Most counseling offices choose to keep costs low, so they might not invest a whole lot in their web presence. They will likely not be ready and waiting to answer your phone calls. Websites should likely give you a way to know a little more about the therapist, whether or not they are licensed, how to contact the therapist, or how to make an appointment. Use this as a tool, and don't solely make your decision based on a website.

5. Ask Questions of the Therapist

It is absolutely fine to call and ask to speak with the therapist. You should be able to ask what they specialize in and how long they have been practicing. It is okay to share what you want to get help with without going into details. For example, you can say you are dealing with depression, anxiety, marriage issues, parenting issues, etc., without going into details. A good therapist will be able to tell you if this is their area of specialization or be able to make recommendations to a person who specializes in this area.

6. Evaluate Your First Appointment

I tell clients on our first meeting that I want them to walk out of the door (or log off) at the end of their first session thinking three things; I want them to be able to say that their counselor...

> *...gets where I am.*
> *...understands where I want to go.*
> *...seems to have tools to help me get there.*

If these three things are present at the end of your first meeting, then schedule another appointment and continue. If these three things are not present, then you might ask your counselor for a referral to another counselor (it is ok to do this), or repeat the above process. I can imagine that there is a part of you that feels like just accepting whatever a counselor has to offer, but this is your session. If you do not like what you are getting, it is OK to ask for something else. If you go to a restaurant and order chicken, and they bring you steak, you are within your rights to ask for something else. This is the same with your counselor. If you are not able to connect, you can seek somebody else.

Also, if somebody did refer you, do them a favor and let them know how the referral worked out for you. If you had a good experience with a particular counselor, let them know so they can refer others to the same counselor. If it did not go so well, let them know that as well, so they can re-evaluate whether or not to send others to the same person.

Establishing a relationship with a good treatment team requires effort and patience. Therapy practices with psychiatrists, psychologists, and therapists all in the same practice can be a helpful option as everybody is in the same spot, and they all talk to each other. Plus, if you encounter someone in that process with whom you cannot connect, it is a little easier to ask for an appointment with another provider.

Let me repeat this point. If you cannot connect with your provider, it will be really hard to trust your provider. If you can't trust them and don't connect to them, it will be really hard for you to take medicine or follow treatment advice. So, if you cannot connect, for whatever reason, find somebody else. Maybe they have a beard, or they are of a different gender, or their accent reminds you of somebody in your past you would rather not remember, if you know that you can't get past it, move on to somebody else. Now, if you cycle through multiple therapists in an attempt to avoid doing the work, that is a different story. But don't let connection issues with your provider be a roadblock to achieving your goals.

Chapter 8

Don't Let the Seminal Event Define You

So after reading the title of this chapter, you may be thinking... "OK, I will just reclassify this major life-altering event as something else. Great book!". But hang with me for a moment. Take a second and quiet down your gatekeeper because he knows he is about to get slapped! Regroup, take a breath, and relax your body. Find that part of you that is tense, and force it to relax. As we walk through the elements of not allowing your seminal event to define your life, understand that nobody is trying to whitewash your seminal event. It happened and it sucked. I am really sorry it happened. Receive this. It happened and it sucked, and I am really sorry about that. There is no amount of therapy and no amount of legal or illegal drugs that will unhappen your past. There is nothing you or anybody can do to undo or redo the past. (You know that because you have already tried that!) But, there is a chance that if you do the work, and trust me it will be work, you can change your present. And if you change your present, there is a chance that your future will be different. There is no guarantee here, but there is a promise. If you keep doing what you have always done, you will likely get what you always got. So...are you ready to change?

GET SOME PERSPECTIVE

What happened to you seems normal to you, and there is a good chance that you have thought it has happened to everybody. My grandfather was an above-the-knee amputee from WWII. I was about 6 years old before I realized that other peoples' grandpa had 2 legs! It was normal for me. The same man taught me how to ride a bike. He would stand at the top of an inclined driveway and push the bike down the hill (because he could not run beside it), and eventually, I got tired of falling and learned how to ride. I just assumed everybody had the same experience as I did. No matter how awful and messed up you are, what happened to you really didn't happen to everybody else, so a key point here is to get some perspective. Talk to somebody and take a chance to ask if their experience was different from your experience. You don't have to be too vulnerable at this point, but recognize that it will feel vulnerable. You don't have to be blunt about your issue, "Hey, did your dad come in your room when you were 13 and have sex with you...I mean, not that it happened to me or anything. I'm just asking for a friend", but you can talk with somebody and ask, "What was your relationship like with your dad?" Or, "How did you know your parents loved you?".

When you open this door, and you start to recognize that your experience was different from the norm, you are going to experience some emotions. And you are going to experience them intently. It is really fine and healthy to have such a feeling. You have a right to feel angry, sad, frustrated, hurt or any number of other emotions. You may even feel relief or calm because it finally starts to make sense for you. You may have read that last sentence and thought I am crazy, but here is the point; you can feel what you want to feel, but that does not give you carte blanche to act on your feelings. This is where a healthy gatekeeper comes into play. Since you likely do not have this healthy gatekeeper yet, lean onto your close friend or counselor. (If you skipped the section on how to find a good counselor, it is time to go back to the beginning of part two and check that out.)

As you gain perspective that what happened to you was not normal, it becomes the foundation on which you begin to build a healthy gatekeeper. You are not an evil person. You are, however, a person who has experienced some awful things. Everybody in the world did not experience those awful things. For some, knowing this brings relief; for others, this leads to increased frustration. It is not important where your emotional response is at this step, but you need to understand that your experience is unique to you and that your experience was real. It really happened. Though, you did not deserve it. You did not deserve it in the past, and you don't deserve it in the present.

MAYBE THE HURT WAS UNINTENTIONAL

As you gain perspective, you may be confronted with the possibility that your negative experience was not intentionally inflicted on you. This is not to say that the hurt was not real, instead, the person who was most responsible for your pain could have been in pain themself, and your pain was a part of a chain reaction in their life. For example, your dad telling you money was not available to purchase that special item you had been wanting was not an intentional act to set off a chain of events that made you believe you were not worthy of family resources. Dad may have been between jobs and was just trying not to get evicted.

I am going to go a step further, and it may be too soon for you to read this. If you find yourself cussing at me after reading this next part, it's ok to skip it. It may be too soon for you to hear it. But what if your abuser did not intentionally set out to hurt you specifically? What if they were also a victim of abuse, and it has systematically run through your family for many generations. What if they have never done the work you are doing now, and they just thought that type of behavior was just normal and expected? This is not an attempt to minimize your abuse. This is not a plea to excuse your abuser. If justice is available, justice should be delivered. This is not a get-out-of-jail card for your abuser. But it is an eviction notice for your gatekeeper. If your gatekeeper told you that you deserve the abuse and also started telling you to give others in your life the same treatment, it is time to change gatekeepers. If your gatekeeper has told you it was not abuse because you felt pleasure or had an orgasm, it is time to change your gatekeeper.

For some, being confronted with the opportunity to consider that their pain was unintentional is liberating. It allows you to open the door to forgiving those who hurt you because you can begin to see those people as broken people who were going through their own set of issues. For others, the fact that they were hurt unintentionally makes it worse. You have carried this hurt and its effects with you and on you for a long time, and the person who inflicted this pain just did so on a whim. This much pain was just an overflow of the pain somebody else was experiencing.

As you take the chance to redefine your seminal event and look at it from a different angle, learning that the person who causes caused your pain was themselves suffering from intense emotional pain can certainly change your perspective. As you gain perspective, you begin to see that what happened to you was not normal. And while there are certainly times where the pain that was caused to you was a result of an untentional mean action, sometimes, it's not. As you begin to better understand the purpose and reasons behind your seminal event, you get the opportunity to confront the situation from an adult brain. Your adult brain has a lot more functionality and capability than your child-like brain.

I AM NOT BEING PUNISHED; JUNK JUST HAPPENS

When you gain perspective on your seminal event, you can begin to combat that internal gatekeeper with this truth: You did not deserve the treatment. Everything bad that happens in your life is not some coordinated effort to systematically punish you because you are a bad or broken person. And everything negative that happens in your life today is not an extension of some punishment that your gatekeeper has convinced you that you deserve. You are not being punished.

Sometimes, junk just happens. Sometimes, there is just a nail in your tire. It is not an extension of the bully who called you horrible names in middle school. You just ran over a nail. Nobody has conspired against you to delay you by 2 hours. (Despite the fact that a NASCAR pit crew can change 4 tires, fill up the tank, and clean the windshield in less than 17 seconds, it still takes you 2 hours to change a tire, along with a few choices words!) When you open up yourself to the possibility that actions are the result of consequences, it frees you to stay in the moment. (Cue the grounding exercises, more to come on this.) When the circumstance you find yourself in is a result of a decision you made, or maybe a decision that somebody around you made, you get to silence the gatekeeper who wants to make it all about your past. Instead of reinforcing past negative events, when you recognize that sometimes junk just happens, it frees you to deal with the junk at hand.

This is not easy to do. After all, your gatekeeper has been telling you for a lifetime that you deserve all of the bad that comes your way. This is not just a flip-the-switch experience where you suddenly believe and behave differently. This is a conscious choice you have to make to fight against your thoughts. (Remember when it was said this was going to be hard work?). Gaining perspective can be a great start to this journey. Having some support to reinforce the point that you are not being punished can be key. Sometimes, having something visual in front of you that can help remind you that you are not being punished. Maybe that is a notecard you tape to your mirror telling you that you are not being punished. It could be a bracelet you wear that reminds you that you are no longer in chains. Maybe it is something that makes absolutely no sense to anybody else, but to you, it serves as a clear reminder that you are not being punished. It can also help you get the internal thought physically out of your head. Just writing out the unhealthy thought that you are being punished can help you see it and appropriately address it. When it stops being internal, you get a chance to focus on it from a different perspective.

Intentionally placing encouraging people in your life is also really helpful. This is not the pep talk bunch that are great at halftime locker room speeches (I know we are down by 102, but today is the day we lose with pride!), but people who can hear you and feel your pain, who can give you empathy, and at the same time remain positive. People who can see your perspective and also show you a different way of looking at things. People who rarely get discouraged. You can't go to the market and buy these people; you have to search them out. They exist. There are chances that you don't know anybody like this, or at least you don't know that you know anybody like this. Here is an experiment I invite you to try. Ask three people you know separately to tell you the most positive person they know. Then, figure out if you know that person. If not, ask for an introduction. If you are the most positive person they know, more to come on this!

The more you are able to recognize the junk of life as something other than just punishment, you may eventually graduate to the perspective that junk happening in the present might actually be helping you in the future. (I know, crazy talk, right.) Maybe that 2-hour delay in changing your tire saved you from a horrible accident, or perhaps, you forgot to pick up the nails you dropped behind your tire during that DIY project. While there is a supernatural component to part of this, there is a practical application here as well. Perhaps the pain of that morning run keeps you from having a heart attack. Maybe the torture you experienced eating that kale salad versus the moment of ecstasy you would have had from that Krispy Kreme donut lowered your cholesterol. These bring us to our next aspect of not letting the seminal event define you.

CONSEQUENCES ARE NOT PUNISHMENT, STOP THE BLAME GAME

Sometimes, life just happens. There is nothing you can do to avoid or prepare for it. It is just junk that happens. Other times, negative experiences come your way as a direct result of some pretty jacked-up choices that you have made. We are now entering a narrow path. You might be thinking, "Duh, I make a bad decision, I have a bad consequence...kinda sounds like a punishment?!?". Yes, while this might be true, for this to lead to future productivity, the key difference here is recognizing the negative consequence of the decision you just made, not a punishment for your past. As discussed earlier, it is about staying in the present and not letting the past take the blame for the situation that is happening now. This is what separates a consequence from a punishment. It may sound like I am splitting hairs, but the difference is monumental. If you are able to recognize that the unpleasant consequences you are experiencing are a direct result of your actions, then you can do something about it! If the negativity in your life is there due to other people's influence on your life, then you are just stuck receiving the bad.

If you are getting ready to make this step, let me issue a warning. On some building doors, there is usually a sign beside that says, "Warning, Exit Only, No Re-Entry". If you are about to make this step towards your healthier future, be aware that there is no entry back into the old way of think-ing. Your gatekeeper knows this, and he's likely screaming at you to walk away from this door because he knows he can't pull you back from this. You may not be ready for this yet, and there is no pressure on this end. You have had too many people try and pressure you into things you did not want to do. Feel free to keep reading to see what the rest of the journey looks like, but know that this is a step you will have to take in order to change your present and eventually change your future. The reason for this will come next. It has the potential to sound really harsh, but this is not the intent. When you begin to own this truth, you gain the power to change.

Once you begin to recognize that your situation is a result of your decisions, you can no longer blame others for your problems.

Let that sink in for a bit. Take a moment, go for a walk, and let the gatekeeper have his rant because this might be his last. Right now, he is telling you that I have no idea what I am talking about, and I have not been through what you have been through.

> Of course, I can't have a healthy relationship with a man after what my dad did to me.
>
> People who experience the level of gaslighting I ex-perienced don't have loving, trust-filled relationships.
>
> I have been watching pornography longer than I have been shaving, there's no way I can have a normal sexual relationship with one woman.
>
> If you had the experience I had with food, you would be in the physical condition I am in too.

Did your gatekeeper get it all out? Are you still ticked at me? If so, take a moment to calm yourself down and read the rest of the section before making up your mind. You need to be in a place where you can think rationally to understand this. Take a self-inventory and see what part of your body is now tense. Then, take a deep breath and force yourself to relax whatever is tense. Go ahead and do it. Take a deep breath, and un-tense whatever you have tensed. Release your breath slowly and completely. Do it again. As we continue, keep doing it.

It is hard to hear logic and exercise logic when your emotions have highjacked your brain. For so long, you have conditioned yourself, or maybe you have been conditioned to believe that the disappointments in your life presently are a direct result of past negative experiences. And while it is true that your past may have sucked, and it may be a good reason why you think and act the way you do, it does not have to define your present and control your future. When you know that your current situation directly results from your actions, you can then recognize that you and you alone can change your actions. The flip side of this is that once you turn the corner to make yourself the sole person responsible for your situation, you can't blame your life (or lack thereof) on somebody else.

Let's face it; it is really easy and convenient to blame others for our problems. If we can blame others, we don't have to take personal responsibility. Blaming others means that we don't need to change. We are perfect; it is other people who have issues. That cop was just out to get me! It didn't matter; I was going 35 miles over the speed limit. It's the cop's fault. If my wife had been ready on time, I would not need to speed, so it's her fault. As long as I can blame others, I don't need to change.

But the more I blame others, the more I push others away. And the more I blame others, the more I give up control over myself to others. My reactions result from my decisions, not the automatic responses to someone else's behavior. As you start to understand that your situation is on you, it can be overwhelming.

You likely did not start making poor decisions with negative consequences yesterday. There are chances that you have been doing this for a while. If making poor life decisions were an Olympic game, you would have a few medals around your neck! You are really good at making bad decisions. It is easy to come up with your acceptance speech at the bad-decision Olympics. You could graciously blame (I mean credit) all of the people who messed up with your life as contributing to your spectacular success at being a failure. But if these are all a result of your decisions, well, that is just depressing. And who wants to be depressed?

So as you wrestle with this idea that you may be experiencing the consequences of your actions, it can be a little much at first. Let's say for a moment you concede that what I am saying is true, and you are the reason you are isolated, addicted, in a messed up relationship, or broke and in debt because of decisions you have made. My guess is that you did not set out to make bad decisions intentionally. You probably thought you were making really good decisions, and it is just those other people who really messed everything up. Wait... you did it again. So a really good question to ask yourself might be, "How can I know that I am actually making good decisions? After all, I don't have a history of making good ones."

Simply asking this question and being aware enough to consider that your decisions may be part of the problem is a great place to start. As you go through this journey, the next question I want you to consider is how much influence you had in your circumstances. You likely did not have much influence if you are stopped at a stoplight and another car rear-ends you. But if you knew your brake lights were out, there is a chance you had a part to play in it. Your problems may not be as simple as an auto accident (who would have thought that phrase would ever make sense).

But let's investigate what influence you have on the decisions you make. One that comes to mind is how consciously you were of the historical trends connected to your decisions. Let's put this in the context of a relationship, for example. When we talk about historical trends, basically, it is asking yourself what you know about the man you are dating before you started dating him? If he had a few prison tattoos, a couple of different STI's, and he does not act surprised when a string of random children call him daddy, this is what we would call a trend. Expecting this person to act differently from their past trends is highly unlikely unless they can verify they have been through some proven change process. If your ticket to financial freedom involves spending all available resources on the lottery instead of establishing a consistent budget and savings plan, this is what we call a trend. There is a good chance that this trend has led to being broke and in debt. If you go to work, make a point of not speaking to people, and go quietly and quickly to your home, lock the doors and close the blinds, this is a trend. It is likely contributing to your isolation and loneliness. If you are depressed and lack motivation, or anxious, and fear is keeping you from acting, and you have been to get help, this is also a trend. Depression and anxiety are highly unlikely to magically disappear. You influence how you get treatment, but if the trend is to avoid treatment, this is a good place to identify that you are experiencing the consequences of your actions. I am not saying that depression, anxiety, bipolar, or any other mental or medical conditions are your fault, but not getting help to treat them is. You have influence over your treatment, and the whole point of this book is to help you realize that you do have the power to get better. That gatekeeper who is telling you just to stay like you are needs to be slapped. The gatekeeper will not help you get better. Only you can do that.

Past trends are one area to address when considering how much influence you have over your current situation. A second area to look at is the present actions. In a relationship, for example, past trends might point to a perfectly healthy person. Previous partners speak of him treating them with respect and dignity. He has demonstrated responsible behaviors in the past. But presently, this person has turned to substances, has become abusive, or is cheating on you. While you cannot control their actions, you can control how much you will allow yourself to be exposed to these negative actions. Most marriage vows include the phrase, "love, honor and cherish", but what I am proposing is that it is not loving, honoring or cherishing (if that is a word) to allow someone to continue on a path of self-destruction. If they are confronted and refuse to admit to their need, setting limits on how much you will be involved in their destruction is entirely up to you. Let's take this out of relationships and turn into finances. If you have made an investment, and all the past trends state that this type of investment is going to yield a profit, but the further you get into the investment, the more money it seems to be losing, at some point, the present loses represent a fact that simply cannot be ignored: this is a bad investment. Do I continue to stay connected to a bad investment and lose even more money, or cut my losses and move on? This is very cut and dry when dealing with an investment, but it can get way more complicated when it is a relationship, a job, or maybe even a family member.

This is where finding a good support system is crucial. If this is not naturally in your sphere of influence, this is where you might seek help from a professional. This could be a mental health counselor, a personal trainer, a financial advisor, a life coach, or anyone who can help you accomplish your goals. It could mean investing in books, podcasts, online videos or some other means of acquiring new information. When you get a different perspective, recognize that consequences are not punishments, and better understand past trends and current actions, you can start making decisions to change your life. But, even when we make new decisions in the present, we have to stop the bad from continuing to happen.

IT'S MY RESPONSIBILITY TO STOP THE BAD FROM HAPPENING TO ME

Nothing in life can access anger in me more than a backed up and especially an overflowing toilet. First off, the problem can be easily prevented. Just put less toilet paper in the toilet or flush more frequently. As a child, my wife lived in a community where rocket engines powered the flusher in the bathroom. From what I have concluded, she could place a small tree in the toilet, and when she pressed the flush handle in her childhood home, whatever was placed in the toilet was chipped up and shot out at warp speed into the sewer system. When we purchased a home together, this home apparently lacked this extreme flushing feature. So, we would frequently have issues where the toilet would back up. (Clearly, this was the problem of the toilet, the cold weather, the expanding toilet paper and not her...oh wait.) In moments of mild stress, like when the toilet is overflowing, panic would overcome my wife, and she would stand in the bathroom screaming my name, watching soiled water flow over the rim of the toilet she had repeatedly flushed.

As I would enter this little self-caused chaos bomb, I would hear the terror in her voice, see the panic on her face, and observe water overflowing the toilet. She would typically say something to the effect of, "The toilet is over-flowing, you gotta fix the clog!". And because I grew up on the other side of the proverbial tracks, and this was not my first rodeo with normal, non-luxury plumbing, I would reach instinctually for the shut-off valve and stop the water flow!

So why the long self-disclosing tail that is probably going to get me in trouble? You have to recognize that it is your responsibility to stop the bad from happening. You alone have to turn off the water to make it stop overflowing. You could choose to go get some towels, reach for the shop vac, and go grab the plunger, but if you don't first shut off the water, the problem is just going to keep growing.

Maybe your bad happened a long time ago, and your seminal event is over and you are just living with the after-effects. But perhaps your seminal event is still happening. If it is, you have to take responsibility to stop it. Maybe the event is over, but the echoes of that event have left you in a situation where you actively invite the bad to continue to come. If this is the case, you have to take the responsibility to stop it.

Let me flesh this out a little more. As an example, let's say you were abused as a child. While your abuser is no longer alive, you have opened yourself up to abusive relationships, and your current partner is actively abusing you. If this is you, then you alone have the responsibility to stop it. (Note that we said "take responsibility", and not to just simply stop it. More to come on this in a moment). Maybe you have been addicted to pornography since the age of 12, and you are 32 now, 10 years into a marriage, actively sneaking pornography and wondering why your wife is emotionally distant. You and you alone have the responsibility to address your sexual addiction. Perhaps you were encouraged to have an unhealthy relationship with food, and you are finding yourself severely unhealthy physically as an adult. You and you alone have the responsibility to change it.

"Oh, is that it? I just say no? Why didn't I think of that? If that's all there is to it, then I am wasting my time reading this book!" Ok, glad you got that out? Taking responsibility is often much more complex than just saying no. There are no snap-out-of-its here. Taking responsibility does place the ownership of the problem with you, and it is up to you to make changes. Nobody will make those changes for you. Nobody but you can fix you. Also, know that you may not be able to do this alone. You will need a team.

Despite being an accomplished college-educated woman, my wife cannot think to turn off the water when the toilet is overflowing. (She also lacks the capacity to portion out the amount of toilet tissue she uses and flush periodically, but I am working really hard to let this go...) But since she caused the problem, it is her responsibility to go and get help for that which she cannot do on her own. When you begin to see that you need a change, you need to assemble your team, consisting of people with abilities that you do not have.

You might be thinking this is a foreign concept, but you do it every day. When you get fuel for your vehicle, do you dig a hole in the ground, extract raw crude oil, take that to a lab, and refine it until you get at least an 87 octane level of purity, and then place that in your car? No, you just have to go to a gas station and pay and put refined crude oil that has been transported to a receptacle near you. Sometimes, you assemble a team to help you out of pure convince even though you do have the capacity to make things for yourself. Do you ever go to a restaurant? You know how to make a meal, but sometimes you just don't want to, so you go and find other professionals to make the same meal you could make, but you just don't want to be inconvenienced.

On a daily basis, unless you are on some pioneering reality TV show, you rely on others to do what you are ultimately responsible for. If you can rely on professionals to bring you food, refine your gas, cut your hair, polish your nails, change your oil, entertain you, etc., it stands to reason that you can also allow others to help you stand up for yourself and take responsibility to stop the bad in your life.

Kicking your abusive boy/girlfriend out of the house may require the backup of local law enforcement. And it is fine and healthy to use the support. Having the strength and confidence that you are not going to be alone and miserable when that abusive person that you are connected to leaves may require the help of a support group or therapist. Undoubtedly, going to a meeting will help you stop the addiction. A sponsor, therapist, and a local computer expert to install a robust internet filter and monitoring system might be necessary to help you stop your addiction. So, build a team of people who can help you accomplish what you are ultimately responsible for.

Taking responsibility does not mean that you will go at it alone, but that you open yourself up to the idea that nobody else is going to change this for you. For too long, your gatekeeper has told you that there is nothing to be done; just accept it. It's time he gets slapped! You can do something about it. You can close the gate. You do not have to keep allowing this bad to continue to enter your life. And just because you can't close that gate by yourself does not mean that you are not responsible for closing it. Nobody is going to take responsibility for you and your problems.

When you gain some perspective on your past and begin to learn that bad things are not punishments but rather the consequences of poor decisions, you learn to accept that sometimes junk just happens. Along this journey, you will learn how to stop the bad and pretty soon. You can start to see that your past is a good reason for why you are where you are/were, but it can no longer be the excuse to stay this way.

THE PAST IS AN EXPLANATION, NOT AN EXCUSE

This section has been all about how not to let your seminal event define you. For a very long time, you have refused to allow yourself to change because your gatekeeper made you believe you don't deserve anything different. After all, when you have a past, just like you have, you can't expect a different future.

Hopefully, by now, you have figured out that statement is just plain false. Your past is certainly a part of you. It has shaped your worldview. But, you and you alone are responsible for you. As you learn not to let your seminal event define you, it ceases to be a seminal event, and it just becomes an event. Remember, nothing is going to undo it. But you get the opportunity to determine what you do with it. You get to decide whether you will continue to allow this event to define you or if you take back control and responsibility and use it as fuel to change your present.

When you tell your story, your past can be a good reason for why you behaved the way you did, but it can no longer be the excuse to stay that way. Instead, it becomes the reason you are becoming the person you want to be. As long as your past is an excuse, you will never take responsibility to stop the bad, you will continue to blame the past and others for your problems, and you will continue to stay like you are. I know this sounds harsh, but the goal here is to change your present, so you can have a different future. I am sorry for the harshness of the truth bomb, but at this point of the journey, we are deep into the slapping of the gatekeeper, and the gloves have come off. It is no time to hold back now. You are at the beginning of forming a new gatekeeper, and before that old voice starts to remind you that you have tried this earlier – you have bought self-help books, you have talked in veiled terms to your doctor or therapist (more on that in the next section), you have joined the gym, you have engaged the filter, you have prayed to God to stop, and every time, you just wound up right back in the same place, and maybe even in a worse spot. Right now, that gatekeeper is telling you this is for other people;

good people who only have minor problems, and this is precisely when you have to get your slapping hand ready. You really need to shut him up!

Have you tried and failed to achieve results? Good, you have now learned a few areas where you might need additional help. Have you tried and failed to achieve results? Good, you have some history in taking the first steps. Have you tried and failed to achieve results? Good, because it is now clear that you are tired of your past defining you. Do not hang your shoulders and return to the bench. Don't get in your car and go home. Your past no longer has the right to define you.

I am not trying to say this is going to be easy. It is really hard work. You have a long road ahead of you. I don't want to tell you that this will be some vacation of a trip because it is going to feel like hell on earth at times. But here is the deal, this arduous journey you are about to embark on will change your life. Not just your life but the lives of those connected to you and any generations that come behind you. Your decisions right now will impact people for generations to come. That may be a little much for you to comprehend, and it may seem overwhelming. You don't need to focus on the future. In case you have not heard the theme, the goal is not to change the future, the goal is to change the present.

When I work with people who are at this point, I like to help them think through a Three-Tier Goal System. Goal number one is to Survive. What do you have to do to get to the point where you have a reasonable sense of confidence that you will stay alive and be able to do so healthily and consistently. What is it going to take to survive? Whatever that is, do it first. Whoever that involves, make the call. We have to get you stable. It may take some time to get you stable, and it is ok and healthy to take that time to get you stable. This may require a medical leave of absence from work to work on you in an Intensive Outpatient or Partial Hospitalization Program. It may also require that you take on a second job to make ends meet. Step one is to survive.

Once you have survival firmly in your grasp, we skip goal two for now and formulate goal three next. Number three is figuring out what you will be doing when you thrive. What does a growing, developing, healthy, happy you look like? What job will you have? What relationships will you have? What will your finances look like? What will your family be doing? What type of friends will you have? Take a bit of time and dream. When you have a real clear vision of what Thrive looks like, it's time to head back to goal number two, which is your Transition goal.

What will it take for you to thrive? What education will you need? What experiences will you need to have? What things will you need to get rid of? What things will you need to stop? Who will you need to get to help you accomplish this? This is how goal two is created and formed. When you figure out how to survive and what it takes to thrive, you can start making plans to accomplish those goals. It may take some time to survive. If so, do that. Don't worry about thriving until you have confidence in your ability to survive.

As you work this system and set small attainable goals along the way, so you can begin to maintain and sustain progress. Staying focused on those goals is key. If you begin to focus on what you cannot control, you will easily get discouraged and lose hope. But as you focus on what you are able to control, you will make progress. While we are on the subject of goals and progress, let me invite you to think of measuring progress differently. When your goal is big and requires a long time to accomplish, rather than measure it by the results that are slow to come in, measure it instead by the number of activities in which you are actively participating that are necessary for you to achieve your goal. For example, if losing weight was your goal, instead of allowing the scale to be your only measurement device, measure your progress by the number of times you exercised this week, the number of times your calorie intake was under the goal, and by the number of healthy food choices you made this week. Eventually, the scale will catch up. If depression is the problem and feeling better is the goal, measure success by the number of days you consistently took your medication this week, the number of days you showered, and the number of therapy sessions you attended. This is not intended to be an exhaustive list, but hopefully, you can see the point.

When your past has defined you for a long time, change will not come easily or quickly. This is not to say that you should just run away from it because change is going to be hard. Acknowledge that it is hard, be ready to do the work and stay on the path to a healthy present. If you have the right tools to measure your success and you can see that you are engaging in healthy activities necessary to achieve your ultimate goal, you are more likely to stay engaged in the process. Instead of letting your past define you, I want you to see that your past becomes a reason to change, not an excuse to stay stuck.

Chapter 9

Speak Your Mind

After your seminal event shaped your worldview to think of yourself differently, losing your voice solidified this new way of looking at the world as permanent. In the last section, you were given steps to implement to not let your seminal event define you. And now, we need to find your voice.

TURN EMOTION INTO MOTIVATION

You have emotions. It is a part of being human. Do you allow yourself to feel your emotions? All of them? Any of them? When you get the chance to truly experience your emotions, this is great fuel to give energy to the voice that you may have lost some time ago. After a seminal event, it is not uncommon for a voice to just become dormant. Those emotions that you may be trying to ignore or just stuff need somewhere to go. Instead of just stuffing them down or passive-aggressively allowing them to slip out, perhaps let your voice have a turn. Tell somebody how you feel. Express your emotion rather than experience them.

By learning to express your emotions, you get the chance to tell somebody you are angry, rather than just throw something at them. You can tell somebody you are hurt without lashing out and trying to make them hurt like you are hurting. You can express happiness without involving a foreign substance or destructive behavior.

I completely understand that this sounds really uncomfortable, and perhaps it sounds a little beyond where you might be. But that is ok. Take a step back, and give your voice time to grow. You do not have to be an expert to get on this in order to begin time to grow.

LET THE VOICE GROW UP

Nobody expects a baby to eat steak. Adolescents are not given the opportunity to enter into binding contracts without parental consent. It is not until you are an adult that you are expected to make adult decisions. Your voice may also be in the same boat. It might not yet be fully mature. It may need some time and space to develop. What would it look like if you allowed your voice the same opportunity to grow up?

For a moment, let's assume that your voice was lost when you were a child, there is a good chance it has not grown at the same pace as your body or even your brain. So when you start to speak up for yourself as an adult, it should not be shocking that your voice sounds like a child or a bratty teenager. As we discuss the various stages of voice maturity, pay attention to where you are on this maturity scale.

When you are a child, your focus is on yourself. Think of a baby who is hungry. He does not exactly know why there is pain or what to call the pain; he just knows something is wrong. He does not care that it is the middle of the night and mom and/or dad need some sleep; he just knows there is some sort of pain, so he cries. He does not have a word for it, but something is not right, and it is his job to cry until it is fixed. Usually, in the crying out phase, he is unable to fix this for himself. Other people have to be involved in fixing this for him because he is simply not capable of getting his own bottle.

As an adolescent, when you are hurting, you want to make others hurt like you are hurting. When an adolescent get's hungry, he may be capable of preparing his own food, but he may not like his options. It is then somebody else's fault that there is no food in the house. It is Mom's fault for not buying the right brand of snack. It is Dad's fault for eating the last one. It is the sibling's fault for liking a different brand of snack, and we all know that the snack he likes/wants is the only viable option for a snack at that moment. Before we dismiss this as being petty and immature, from a developmental standpoint, an adolescent is in between a child and an adult. There is confusion about how much of life they are supposed to do by themselves and how much they are supposed to be dependent on others. There is a simultaneous drive for independence and a desire to be provided for. If it sounds confusing to you, try experiencing it as an adolescent! When your voice is in adolescent mode, it knows what it wants. It knows how to name it, but it does not know how to attain it, or even if it has permission to attain it. Instead of making a plan to fix the problem, the adolescent voice tends to make everybody else aware of their problem, with the hopes that their problem will become somebody else's problem, and then somebody else will fix it for you.

As an adult, you can look at the pain you are experiencing, figure out where the pain is coming from, and devise a plan to stop the pain and heal yourself. If you are hungry, you can look in the fridge or pantry, see if there is something acceptable for you, then prepare your own meal. If food is not available there, you can either order it, go to a restaurant, or run to the grocery store. Either way, as an adult, you have options, and you have permission to exercise one of those options. At the end of it, nobody else will be providing food for you. If you are a hungry adult, it is up to you to find food.

So, if you are just starting to feel your emotions, and the only way you can express it is to talk about how hurt you are or how messed up or unfair a situation is, in the beginning, this is both normal and expected. After all, your voice is still a toddler. But what is not ok is to remain a toddler. Your voice needs a place to grow. And growth usually requires it to go through adolescence.

When this stage of development hits your voice, you want people around you to feel what you feel. If you are sad, everybody else have to be sad. If you are angry, people around you better be angry too, and if they are not, you know just what buttons to push to try and make them angry. And, if we catch you at just the right time on the right day and in the right mood, you have sniper-like precision in insulting and belittling people. After all, you have received it for so long; it is just part of you. But, as a teenager, when you unleash your assault (either as a verbal assault or a grade-A temper tantrum), it does not take long to feel terrible. It is at this moment that you have a choice to make. You can take it to the extreme and tell your voice that speaking up for yourself is bad, wrong, and evil and is never again allowed to rear its ugly head, or you can own your actions, make apologies, offer amends, and learn from your outburst.

Think of it this way. You need to learn to speak and not yell. When you let emotions build-up, and you finally decide to try out your voice, it is as though you are yelling, not speaking. Yelling is the go-to for a teenager right before they slam a door. While this is not ideal behavior, recognize this as progress. Prior to this, your voice was silent. So the fact that you can yell is an improvement. But, you are capable of more than just yelling. You have the opportunity and the responsibility to properly and effectively communicate. But to do this, you must take responsibility for yourself and your rants.

When you take responsibility for yourself, you give this voice some fuel to grow. There is no promise or guarantee that your voice will sky-rocket into adulthood, but by owning your voice and the responsibilities associated with speaking for yourself, you feed your voice a few nutrients. As you continue to do this, your voice grows into maturity.

A mature voice can assess the situation, and clearly judge what is in your best interest. A decision can be made that resolves the situation, stops the hurt, protects self, and respects the other parties involved. If justice is needed, proper authority can be called. You don't see adults engaged in physical altercations; they work out problems with lawyers!

While you may have a more mature voice around certain topics or certain people, the maturity level of your voice can be drastically different around others. At work, you may be an adult. You are a problem solver. Your coworkers respect you, and you know how to deliver the goods. But when you get home, you might feel like a little girl around your husband. Or when you visit family, that strong, confident adult suddenly becomes a little child. Avoiding your husband or avoiding your family may not be the best answer. Allowing your voice to grow might be. Allowing your voice to grow in all areas of your life will be a key to long-term success and allow you to keep your gatekeeper in check. If he has room to silence your voice in one area of life, he will likely try and expand his territory. If you are not confident at home, he will seek any chance he can to build upon that insecurity and derail your confidence at work.

Giving your voice time to grow will be essential for you to develop a voice that is good for you and good for society. For your voice to be heard, it may be necessary to quiet the other voices in your life.

QUIET THE OTHER VOICES

Have you ever listened to a choir? It can be hard to hear one individual's voice while scores of people are all singing at the same time. When it is a good choir, everybody won't be singing the same note. They are harmonizing together and making beautiful music. If you have a choir of 100 people, and 1 person is not singing, it is really hard to tell. If that same person starts singing but is just a little off, it's not that bad. You can still hear the other voices in the choir, and you may not even know that there is a voice that is off. But, when everybody stops, and that one voice keeps singing, then that off-voice becomes noticeable.

When you start to find your own voice, there are likely many other voices in your life who have an opinion about what your voice should be saying. Most of the time, at this phase in the process, those voices are pretty unhealthy.

When your voice starts speaking, it can easily get lost in the choir of people around you, or most of the time within you, saying something else. Sometimes, that is all the same thing, other times, each of those voices are all saying something different. But all of the time, those voices are not your voice. In order to have your voice heard, it is necessary to quiet the other voices in your life.

What does this look like? This could be as simple as distancing yourself from unhealthy people. But this may not be so simple, especially if these are the only people in your life. I learned a long time ago that people would choose to stay connected to unhealthy people versus being disconnected from unhealthy people and living in isolation. So before you start to distance yourself from unhealthy people, it may be necessary to first identify and connect with healthy people. When you start to separate from the unhealthy voices, you have a safe place to land.

But, separating yourself from unhealthy voices can become more complicated when you can't cut those voices out of your life. What if they are parents, spouses, children, or business partners you can't just leave? Maybe your overall existence is tied to theirs at this point, and separating from them will bring actual harm to your life. This is where healthy boundaries come into play. Being able to protect yourself while still going about your life is key. Think of it this way. If you were a nurse and cared for a patient with an infectious disease, you may have to wear gloves, put on a mask, and possibly a gown before entering the patient's room. You still go into the room to do your job, but you have the specialized gear to help you stay safe and healthy so you can continue to do your job. Boundaries work in a similar way. They allow you to go into hostile environments and exit them healthily. The works of Henry Cloud and John Townsend are awesome and very practical. I highly recommend you check out their book Boundaries.

As you grow your voice, you will eventually get the chance to create greater strength in your life and eventually not be as tied to these unhealthy people. But at this point, let's not worry about that. As you put some distance between you and the unhealthy voices in your life, you can give your voice the time and space it needs to grow. Like a plant in need of some TLC, it takes time to absorb the nutrients. It is good to give yourself time to grow and develop your voice. If you find yourself overwhelmed by all of the voices in your life and feel like you can't get a word in for yourself, try writing down your voice. Share these writings with your therapist. Use that session to grow your voice. Join a support group that will allow you to speak for yourself. Go to a recovery meeting. You might need to record voice memos on your phone, or you could just call yourself and leave yourself a message. Just do something to get your voice out and allow it to be heard, particularly be heard by you.

When you do this, take a moment to feel how it feels to speak for yourself. Soak it in. But don't get discouraged because those other voices are pretty good at shutting you down. The first couple of times you speak your voice, expect some opposition. It is very likely that the voice stealers and the voice suppressors will step up their game. It is then that your gatekeeper will try to tell you how pointless it is to speak up for yourself. *Just go ahead and keep quiet. Nobody wants to hear you anyway. There is no point in experiencing all of this pain and rejection so that you can say something that nobody wants to hear....* It's time to get your gatekeeper knocked into line. Don't take his bait anymore. Grow from the experience, figure out where in the exchange you could not continue speaking for yourself and put some tools into place to help you next time. It will get easier with practice.

So what are these tools? First, take some time to internally know your likes and preferences. Even if you do not externally express your internal voice, knowing what you want and don't want, what you like and don't like can be powerful, especially if others have been telling you what you want and don't want for most of your life. Taking a moment and allowing yourself to speak up to yourself is a good first step. This may sound easy, and you may think that you already know what you like and don't like, but you may find this more difficult than you think. What restaurants do you like? Have you ever been able to pick, or has somebody else just told you where to go? What music do you like to listen to? What activities do you like to do? Do you have a hobby? Do you enjoy doing it, or did somebody tell you to do it and you just kept doing it? What is your favorite shirt? What is your dream car? If you could go on vacation tomorrow, where would you go? Who would you take with you? Do you like dogs or cats? This might sound simple or even a little silly, but don't be surprised if you struggle with this. It is good and healthy to take some time to figure out what you really like and want.

A second tool is to get your voice out. As discussed above, this is best done in a safe environment. This will likely not be a confrontation with a voice stealer, instead, you will be practicing externalizing your internal voice in a safe environment. Safe environments can be a therapy session or in a support group. It could be with trusted friends, or total strangers who you are not close enough with and can't hurt you. It may start out as a journal entry, or it may also be in a trusted or safe online forum that is free of internet trolls. The goal here is not so much that you have to fully embrace the power of your voice but that you give it a test drive and just experience what it is like to tell somebody what you like or want. Maybe you go to a restaurant and ask the server to bring you exactly what you want. Then, when they bring it, change your mind and ask for something different. Order a soda, then ask for tea. Just practice what it feels like to ask for something and then actually get it.

A third tool is backup. Backup is different than getting lost in the crowd. Backup happens because you are the star of the show. You are singing the lead part, and they are there to harmonize with you and make sure you sound good. They are not competing for center stage; they know their place. Interestingly enough, in most major shows, the backup singer is typically a better musician than the star. They have a better range and have been better trained, but they are not there to take the spotlight; they are there to simply provide backup. Your backup may be better able to communicate for you, they may have more experience communicating than you do, but good backup stays behind you while you belt it out in the spotlight. Good backup can be a counselor, a friend, or some other supportive person in your life. It can also be a book or a podcast that arms you with confidence.

A fourth tool is to know your audience. While we could talk about how the style of communication may change from person to person, I am more concerned with whether the audience will receive your communication. If the person you are communicating with has made it clear they will not listen to you, part of growing your voice is not wasting it. Spending time and energy talking to someone who will not listen to you does not help your voice grow, instead it weakens it. I know that this fourth tool is confusing. It sounds like I am telling you just to be quiet and not speak. But I am not. If the only audience you have does not want to hear your voice, it may be time to change audiences, not relinquish your voice. Changing audiences is not always easy, but it gives you the opportunity to express yourself around people who love and care about you. They are quiet when you speak instead of trying to shut you down and boo you off the stage.

Using these tools will not be easy at first. They will feel awkward the first couple of times you take them out of the box. Don't let this discourage you. Don't give in to your gatekeeper and put them back into the box. Keep working. It will take time for your voice to grow and develop, and it is acceptable to get some lessons along the way. Keep taking the small steps. Growth typically involves some sort of pain. But this pain is different than the pain you have experienced previously. That pain just led to injury, whereas this pain leads to healing and growth. Soon, you will be singing a solo and the choir behind you will either serve as backup, or will just have to be quiet because they just can't keep up!

Chapter 10

The Fair Comes in October

"Yeah, but what about all these other people who never have to deal with any of this crap. It just really sucks that I have to do all of this work. It's just not fair!" In the south where I grew up, we had a saying, or more like a say'n. The fair comes in October. If you want fair, we will buy you some tickets and you can eat some really unhealthy food that tastes great and ride a ride put together and operated by a guy who has been under the influence of marijuana since the third grade, which was also his last year of formal education. Until then, suck it up buttercup (sorry, southern phrases are now flowing) and get to it. Life is not fair.

When your gatekeeper gets threatened and confronted, he does what any unhealthy and immature communicator does in an argument; he tries to blame somebody or something else. He feels threatened and attacked, and instead of facing the reality that he might be part of the problem, he convinces you that because life is not fair, because others do not have to deal with the same problems you have to deal with, because others have not had the same past experiences you have had, that it's not his fault. It's their fault, or the world's fault, or God's fault, or anybody-but-his's fault, and therefore, you need to keep listening to your gatekeeper and stay stuck where you are.

When you start to recognize the reality that this world is not fair, that it was never supposed to be fair, and that you were never promised fairness, you can stop using this as an excuse to stay stuck and start owning your problems and start moving forward. But how did we get here? How and why is it so easy to believe that fairness is some God-given-American right? Let's explore this subject for a bit. There are philosophical arguments and discussions beyond this scope, but let's at least stir the pot for a bit.

PARTICIPATION TROPHIES

For the Millennials among us, you likely grew up in a world where everybody got the same reward no matter how, when, or where they finished the contest. Participation trophies became popular because nobody wants to feel like a loser, especially if you finished last! Everybody should get a trophy because nobody is supposed to be better than anybody. Soon, we just stopped keeping score for sporting events because the goal was not winning but building teamwork and developing self-esteem.

I am a counselor. I really want people to be able to work well with others and have healthy self-esteem. I agree that these are really valuable for healthy adult functioning. And I get the sentiment behind giving everybody something and not encouraging people to feel bad that they might not have done well as somebody else. However, some took this to extremes. Here, we understand that everybody is equal and all capable of achieving whatever they want. We held these truths to be self-evident that all men are created equal and endowed by their creator with certain unalienable rights!

But the reality of this is just not true. By nature of genetics, some people have bodies that are capable of running really fast. Other people are just a whole lot bigger than the rest of us. Some have minds that can comprehend complex equations at the age of 4 that most of us still can't figure out with college degrees. People are just different. You are different from everybody else.

Beyond genetics, some people grow up in environments that afford them way more opportunity and privilege than others. There is a reason why certain families stay in political and financial power for generations. It's not that they are better people; it is more about the nurture they have received along the way. Generations before them paved the way for their offspring to be senators, governors or presidents. When grandpa started the business and made it big, he afforded dad the chance to go to college and take the company public, and the son gets chances of advancement that the guy off the street does not get simply because of bloodlines and because of the training son has received along the way.

To try and pretend that everybody can do exactly what they want and all can get the same reward is unfortunately not true! Some people have it better than you, and other people have it worse than you. Some people had loving parents, and some people had horrible abusive parents. Some people go home after school and just focus on homework and after-school activities, while others went home and tried not to get raped each night. It is horribly unfair. I am really sorry you have had to put up with the junk that you lived through. You should not have had to deal with that. But the person who had secure attachments and a safe environment is not to blame for your crappy childhood. And guess what, neither are you. It was not your fault. There is a small chance that it was not your abuser's fault. Your abuser could have also been the victim or somebody else who was the victim of somebody else, and this could have been going on for generations. Even if it is your abuser's fault, it's still not your fault. While you may not have had a choice to stop it, you do have a choice not to pass it along. You cannot change your past, but you can change you, which will change your future and the future of future generations coming in front of you. Even if you don't have nor ever plan to have kids, the world can be different because of you.

I am not saying the unfairness of life is a good thing or even a bad thing. I'm just simply pointing out that it is a thing. People are different. They have different capabilities. They have different aptitudes. They have different interests. I don't think that the founding fathers of the USA wanted everybody to be the same, rather, they wanted everyone to have the same opportunity. At the time of its writing, the Declaration of Independence was not true. There were entire categories of people to whom the promise of equality did not apply. People of color and people with vaginas were not granted basic voting rights for many years after these first statements were penned. Basically, I am saying that there is a difference between fair and just.

UNJUST VS. UNFAIR

You may find yourself in a situation where you are struggling with injustice. You are being treated differently than your coworker. The laws and rules that apply to you might not apply to her. This goes beyond fair, and it gets into justice. Justice should be fair. The law should judge all people the same, regardless of race, religion, gender, or sexual orientation. It is right and healthy to be bothered by injustice. But it may be hard to separate the two. Let me give you some examples that might help.

Let's say you work in sales. Each month, your coworker sells 100 units while you sell 75. So, your coworker makes more money than you. This is not fair, but it is just. Just because your coworker is a better salesperson than you, arrives earlier, stays longer, and has a larger personal network that they can sell to is not fair, but it is just.

However, if we are in the same scenario and your co-worker is selling more because your boss is constantly giving them referrals because your coworker is sleeping with the boss, this is both unfair and unjust.

If you are an NBA player, and you score 30 points a night, and your teammate scores 37 points a night, this is unfair, but it is just because you are all playing by the same rules. But if your teammate and coach have bribed the official not to call fouls on your teammate to make them have an unfair advantage, it is both unfair and unjust.

Hopefully, the concept is becoming more clear. As you are able to distinguish between unjust and unfair, and you are convinced that you are in an unjust situation, what do you do? Here are a few options you have. 1, stay and fight, 2, leave and fight it, 3, stay and accept it, and 4, leave and let it go. This may sound pretty simplistic, but your options are limited.

If you do choose to stay and fight it, here are a few things to consider. First, fight from a position of strength. Don't engage in a fight that losing might be really unhealthy for you. If you cannot fight from a position of strength, get healthy first before fighting. This might mean a leave of absence from work where you get a chance to work on yourself and develop your personal boundaries. It could also mean leaving a relationship that is unhealthy and harming your life. If this is the case, get to a position of safety. From your safe place, engage in the fight if you need to. Second, if you choose to stay and fight, fight justly. Resist the urge to compromise yourself and your integrity to win the battle. If you are going to fight injustice, fight from a position of strength and fight it the right way. It may take longer, but the victory will be more satisfying and complete. Third, fight with healthy people. If it is necessary to involve others in the fight, be aware of the people you bring into the battle. Don't go to battle with people you cannot trust.

There are times when the best way to fight injustice may require you to leave to fight it. You simply may not be safe to stay in the situation and fight. Remember, you need to fight injustice from a position of strength. If you cannot get to strength by staying where you are, get safe and then fight the injustice. Confronting your abusive spouse may not be a safe act to do while you are still in the home. This does not mean that you leave and just pretend it did not happen, but you leave home, and fight the injustice from a position of safety.

There are some injustices that might not be appropriate or logical for you to fight. You just might not be able to win. And even if you win, it might not actually benefit you that much. If this is the case, staying and accepting it may be the best option. This would be for injustices that are not creating significant harm in your life. These would be injustices that are more in the annoyance category or those injustices that simply cannot be fought. If fighting the battle will not solve the injustice and it will not improve your life or your situation, accepting the injustice and continuing with your life may be the best option. For example, maybe your dream school wants to charge you $225,000 for a degree to land you a job making $37,000 a year? The cost of this education may not be fair or just, but trying to fight with the institution to lower the costs for you may not be practical. It may be easier to go to community college and a state school for that job than to go to school and leave with a house-sized debt that you can never repay to fight the man.

However, if the injustice is harming you, and it cannot be fixed, or it is outside of your responsibility to fix it, it may just be good to move on and let it go. If your partner is constantly watching porn, and expects you to act out unrealistic fantasies and berates you when you fall short of the fake reality on the screen, it is both unjust and unfair. But trying to force someone into treatment they don't want may not be worth the fight. It may be safer and healthier for you just to move on. The fact of your departure may be more of a blow to the injustice than you staying and trying to fight it. Sometimes, the fight is just not win-able. You can win some battles, but the cost of that battle is so great you lose the war. So take stock at the beginning and figure out if the battle for justice is worth it.

You might need to get some outside help in determining how you should deal with the injustices you are facing because you may not be able to see this for yourself due to the emotions involved. This is where your support team comes in. Their unbiased insight can help you determine if the fight is worth fighting or if you are fighting a losing battle. They can help you with resources to stay and fight healthily or resources to exit the situation and appropriately fight the injustice. They may be the support you need to leave an unhealthy situation and provide you with a space to mourn and grieve your loss and allow you the strength to move on.

IS EQUALITY FAIR?

This is a big debate. There are times when keeping all things equal is not just. If I have a handicap that requires me to use a wheelchair, it is not just to deny me a job that I am perfectly capable of doing because there is no ramp access to the building. But keeping me in that job when I start sucking at it because you have spent a bunch of money on a wheelchair ramp, and you are afraid of a lawsuit if you terminate my employment is also unfair and unjust.

Our society has a long way to go to achieving liberty and justice for all. The point here is to recognize that life is not fair. If there is something you can do to bring justice to your situation which will allow you to be successful, and you can do it from a position of strength and protection, do it. But to refuse to engage in helping yourself simply because others have an unfair advantage is self-defeating and keeps your gatekeeper in power. Remember, we are here to slap him, not to help him grow. He has had an unfair and unjust control of your mind long enough.

Chapter 11

Needing Help is Human

All of this might be getting you to the point where you might be thinking, "He's going to tell me to ask somebody for help, and I just don't do that!" Well, here we are. Needing help makes you human. In fact, getting help from fellow man has allowed the human race not to get eaten by other more capable predators. Because our ancient ancestors were able to band together, communicate with each other, and ask each other for help, the various animals who would find us tasty were kept at bay. However, sometimes, asking for help may bring up some pretty painful experiences. I want to walk through the process of how asking for help may have been corrupted for you and see if we can map out a solution.

As kids, particularly as infants, we need help. Without help, we could not feed ourselves, clean ourselves, or even move out of the path of danger. We asked for help the only way we knew; we cried until we got whatever was needed to satisfy the hunger, the discomfort, or the desire we were experiencing. As we grew and our vocabulary grew, we continued to ask for help. But perhaps there came the point when you were blocked from asking for help. Similar to what we discussed when somebody took your voice, perhaps asking for help involved some sort of shame or judgement. When phrases like, "How many times do I have to tell you?", or "Only stupid people would ask a stupid question like that" became the response to your request, you put up a wall and begin to teach yourself that asking for help is some form of weakness. While you may not have fully lost your voice here, you certainly learned that asking for help specifically was not allowed. There may have been subtle teachings that if you need help, you are somehow less-than.

Or, maybe you got help when you asked for it, but you got more than you bargained for. Asking for help could have meant that you will get more than you asked for. Was asking for help conditional in your world? That is, you could ask for it, but you owed somebody in return when you received it. If so, you may have quickly learned that these transactional encounters are rarely fair. And if your gatekeeper only allows you to give out good and not ever ask for anything in return, there is a good chance that you have been taken advantage of in the giving vs. receiving of help. Therefore, you constantly have an alert sounding in your brain when it is time to ask for help.

Help may have involved some sort of lecture about how you should have already learned this or should already have the help you are asking for. And who wants to hear a lecture when you really need some help? If your arm is broken, you don't need a safety lecture about how you could have prevented a broken arm; you need some painkillers and a cast. You likely know full well, maybe even better than the lecturer, how stupid the decision was that got you into the place where you needed help in the first place. Nonetheless, you are here now and in need of help. You want to say, "Can I just heal for a bit and stop this stabbing pain? Then I might be able to hear the lecture better?"

Maybe you have had the experience that the help you are wanting is not the help that others are willing to give. Maybe you really want what you are asking for, but other people assess your situation and determine you really need something different. Let's flesh this out a bit. Let's say you are doing laundry, and your washing machine breaks mid-cycle. And you call a friend and ask if you can come over to do laundry at their place. Your friend says no, but he would be happy to help you fix your washing machine. At that moment, you don't want your washing machine fixed, you have wet clothes you need to wash so you can get to work, but your friend has a point, you need to get your washing machine fixed. This is a simple example, but perhaps it is better applied to finances. Perhaps you have a bill that is due, and you need money to pay your bill, and you reach out for help. Instead of giving you money, the person on the other side gives you a book on finances and offers to help you set up a budget. The help offered is not what you want, but it may be what you need, but you don't want what you need; you want what you want!

You could just be tired to having to prove that you actually need the help that you need. If your need is 'help with mental illness' and nobody in your family believes that such a thing is real or exists, you might just be tired of trying to prove that you have what you say you have just to get help. Only you will ever be able to know how you feel.

Because they have never experienced depression, anxiety, hallucinations, ADHD, or any form of mental illness, they have no idea how it has impacted your life. They would say, "Snap out of it", as though it was that easy. While these people may be the only people at this point in your life who can help you, you rationalize that it is just easier not to get help than to get into a debate that you simply lack the energy to have, and that is unlikely to produce any different results from the last 10 times you had this debate. Did you hear your gatekeeper talking just then?

Depending on factors like ethnicity, gender, religion, etc., some topics are just difficult to talk about. Money, certain personal health issues, sex, addictions, or other similar topics can be taboo in certain cultures. You might really need help, but your gatekeeper has convinced you that nobody wants to hear about this stuff or that these sorts of topics are not proper to talk about. Culture or religion might be telling you that good girls/boys don't talk about such things. They make you believe it is best to keep that to yourself, or even better, just don't think about it at all; maybe it will just resolve itself.

Whatever your obstacles are to getting help, I want you to see them as just that, obstacles. An obstacle is something in your way that you either need to remove or go around. You don't let an obstacle ruin your trip. You are worthy of being helped. Hear this and receive this. You are worthy of being helped. This is not a battle you want to let your gatekeeper win. While it may be true that you might not have the healthiest of help sources in your life right now, take what you can get, and hire what you cannot. A counselor or a doctor is a good place to start. Be honest about what you need, and be open to receiving what they have to offer. Even if what they are offering is not what you thought you needed, take the help that healthy people have to offer. Sometimes, it is so easy to get caught up in the moment that you lose sight of the forest for all the trees. Someone not involved can have a different perspective. It is also good to speak your mind and be assertive with what you need. If medications are not working, it is ok to ask your doctor for something else, and not just keep taking the same medications that do not work, or worse, just stop taking medications because you are fed up with the process. The fact that you are reading something like this is also really good. Get help from available resources. Trusted websites, quality videos or podcasts are great opportunities to get help from somebody without asking. It does not take the place of reaching out to someone, but it may give you the resources to gain the necessary momentum to reach out to somebody and be able to identify and ask for what you truly need. In some cases, you may need to involve law enforcement to help protect you, and this is a good thing to do as well. This is why many police officers go into this field, to protect and serve. No joke, I am good friends with several law enforcement officers, and it is not just a slogan. They really believe it and are pleased and honored to help those in need.

As you continue to slap your gatekeeper into line, it will become easier to identify healthy people in your life, and will be able to grow a healthy network of resources. Growing these resources through healthy relationships is like an insurance policy for any future negative events. You won't have to go through them alone. And, don't be surprised that as these healthy friends ask you for help, you find yourself actually wanting to give it to them, and not feel taken advantaged of when you do.

IT'S OK THAT I AM NOT OK...

No matter what your history is with asking for help, and no matter what your gatekeeper is telling you about asking for help from others, I want you to know that it is OK that you are not OK. I realize that your gatekeeper has formed his position on not asking for help out of good reason. I recognize that there is likely a great deal of pain that he is trying to keep you from re-experiencing, but to not ask for help, you would need all knowledge, all power, and be omnipresent. If you were all of that, people would be lining up to worship you because you would be God!

It is just not rational to think that you will be able to go through life without needing some form of help. Nobody is perfect. I want you to be able to soak this in for a bit. Nobody can do life all by themselves. People need help. Likely, you are willing and able to offer help to others. And you do so out of love and appreciation. But when it comes to asking others for help for yourself, somehow you get repulsed. This is a good time to slap the gatekeeper.

You are worth helping. You are worth receiving help. I can almost hear your gatekeeper cussing you out about now. As we get further down this road and you might consider asking somebody for help, he is likely taking you on a trip down a painful-memory lane. All of the times when you have asked for help in the past will be flashed before you. The guilt, the shame, the pain; they are all on this hellish tour you never signed up for, yet you just keep mindlessly stepping on the bus and putting on the headsets. If you let him, your gatekeeper will steer you right down a path of self-destruction, and if he has his way, you will never get back to this place again. Don't get on that bus. Hang out here for a bit in the land of the slapped gatekeeper!

IT'S NOT OK TO STAY 'NOT OK'

While it is OK not to be OK, it is not OK to stay NOT OK. Needing help is human, but just recognizing that you need help will not get you help. You need to ask for help. Remember what we said about your responsibility to change yourself? This is true, but you don't have to change yourself alone. Others are available to help you. And your gatekeeper has had the last word on help for too long. You are not less of a person when you ask for help. You are not weak when asking for help. There may be people in your life who will tell you such, but they are not the type of people from whom you need to ask for help. These are not helpful people.

But what if you are ok with asking for help, and the person who is the appropriate person you need to ask for help has no desire to give it? Or maybe they don't know how to even offer this support? Remember, it is your responsibility to solve your problem. While the proper channels do not always yield results, you still have the responsibility to achieve your goal. If achieving your goal requires help, and achieving your goal will always require help, if the help you are seeking is not helpful, it is your responsibility to seek additional help. Sure, it might make the person who is "supposed" to be helping you feel bad that they are not helping you, but you are not responsible for their emotions. You are responsible for your actions and your goal. It is OK to seek out additional help. But trust me, your gatekeeper is likely screaming at you at this point. Telling you how nobody can help you, even the people who are assigned to help you can't help you, and you are just beyond help. As you take the next step towards obtaining healthy help, your gatekeeper knows he is getting slapped.

IDENTIFY HEALTHY SOURCES FOR HELP

One of the reasons that previous attempts to gain health ended so poorly could be a direct result of the people from whom you were asking help. It could be that the people you were asking help from were in no position to be giving it. They might be just as deep in the same problem as you are in and have no clue how to get themselves out of it, much less how to help you. Think of it this way, if you are struggling with alcohol addiction, asking your drunk friend at the bar how to get sober is not likely to yield a healthy answer. If you are looking for relationship wisdom to save your marriage, asking the guy at work who has been married 5 times about what to do is probably not going to work, unless your plan is to do the exact opposite of what he says!

Maybe the people who you are trying to get help from are the people who are actually causing the problem. Asking them for help is like asking your abuser for help with a safety plan. Taking a realistic look at finding the source of the pain can help you know who not to ask for help. This sounds easy on the surface but may require some intense digging to uncover the source of your problem. And I want to affirm to you that it is ok that it takes some time to do this. There is no mandate that you have all of this figured out within 24 hours. And it may be that as you address one problem, it leads you to understand that there is another problem under the surface that you never knew was there.

But, there is also a likelihood that there are not too many healthy people in your life at the moment. So it may become important to start identifying where you might find healthy people who can help you, even if they are not currently in a relationship with you. Even if you do not currently need help, it is still a really good idea to identify who you seek help from in key areas of your life.

A medical doctor is often the first line of defense. Being able to actually tell your doctor what is going on and what you are experiencing is really helpful. I know that there is a fear of being judged or shamed, but telling this person what is truly going on with you can be a great source of help. While he/she might not be able to provide all of the help, you can likely receive direction regarding the next step to take. A therapist is also in this boat. Take a chance and tell your counselor what is actually going on. Ask the question you want to be answered. They will not be able to help you with everything, but they can likely help you map out a plan and identify where to go next. You may also find similar help from your house of worship. Talk with your spiritual leader and see who they might recommend you to talk to next. And if you have all three in your life, ask for help from all three. When they all start to give insight and direction, see if there are any points where the help overlaps, then walk with a little bit of confidence down that path.

If you have healthy people in your life, they can also be a good source of help. But I would encourage you to make sure they are actually demonstrating success in whatever area you are seeking help. If you are trying to get help losing weight, don't ask an obese friend for help. If you need help with finances, don't ask a broke friend. Here are a few character qualities to consider when reaching out to a friend or a professional for help.

First, find somebody that can listen to you. Somebody that will actually hear you. If a person is still trying to take your voice from you, they are likely not a good source for help. If you feel heard while with a potential helper, or you notice this person repeating back to you what they heard you say, it is a good chance you have found somebody who can listen. If they are doing multiple other things while you are talking to them, there is a good chance they are not listening. This can be true of a friend, and it can also be true of a doctor or a therapist. If they are not listening, go find somebody else.

Second, this person needs to lead with empathy. If they jump right into barking orders at you, you will probably not feel heard, and you will probably not do whatever it is they say. An empathetic person is willing to just feel what you feel for a moment. This can be overdone, such that all somebody does is empathize, but if done right, it can set the tone for healthy help. If it is not done well, it is unlikely that you will be able to get to number three on this list, which is finding somebody you can trust.

If your potential help cannot hear you and cannot feel what you feel, it is highly unlikely that you will ever be able to trust them. Trust is the ability to create a mental picture of what you think that person is doing or saying when you are not around and then, from time to time, catch them doing what they say they are doing. If somebody says they are at work, and go by their job and see them there or see their car in the parking lot, you grow your trust for that person a bit. When it comes to help, you might try out what they offer, and you see it actually working; the person they recommend you talk to is not a jerk, and the activity they suggest is actually beneficial.

Once you have found a healthy person who can pass these three tests, you need to actually have a plan. It's great that they hear you, feel what you feel, and trust them, but if they have no strategy to get you out of your condition, they will not be much help. They need to clearly communicate that plan in bite-sized chunks that you can actually digest. If they tell you some 34 point plan to get better, you are likely not going to be able to make that happen. Instead, if they can break up their 34 point plan into 17 two-point segments and give it to you a little at a time, you are much more likely to follow through. If they are listening to you, and are empathizing with you, and they have a plan, they should be able to know how much you are willing and able to do at each step along the journey.

These 4 traits are helpful to find in a friend, but they are also necessary to find in a professional. If your pastor or rabbi or priest just talks over you and does not hear you, you are likely not going to trust the advice that comes next. If your doctor never looks up from his laptop during the entire visit, you may need to find a new doctor. If your therapist holds your hand and cries with you but has no plan to get you further down the road, it might be a good idea to get a new therapist.

WHEN TO ASK FOR HELP

It is never too late to ask for help. Your gatekeeper wants you to believe you are beyond help, but it is just simply not true. It is never too late to ask for help. You are helpable. Please do not believe the lie that you have passed the point of no return. Any point along the journey where you are able to ask for help is a good place to ask. But if you are wondering if you are at a place where you need help, here are a few suggestions.

Pay attention to your body. Particularly your ability to sleep. If you go more than three days without sleeping, or you go for three days where all you do is sleep, then it's time to get help. Make an appointment with your medical doctor or psychiatrist, and have a conversation about sleep. Pay attention to any pain that you are experiencing, whether this is physical pain or emotional pain. Your body may be sending you signals that something is not right. This is a good time to seek out help. If your weight or appetite fluctuates and you are gaining weight or losing weight in an unexplained or unexpected way, reach out for help.

Beyond your body, look at your environment. If you are having trouble adulting: your mail is piled up, laundry can't get washed, your car has run out of gas, bills start having red ink on the envelopes, or maybe your place just plain stinks because you have not cleaned or taken out the trash in a while, it's a good idea to seek out some help.

If you are going through a major life transition, even if you are navigating this transition well, proactively (or reactively if you are not doing so well with the transition), seek out help. If you are moving, starting a new job, changing status in your relationship (single to married, together to it's-not-you-it's-me, married to single, married to widow), get some help to navigate this. When a new baby comes into the picture, get some help. You might be doing really well, but it is better to have people on board and not need them than to get down this road and recognize that things are not going so great.

LEARN MY CAPACITY AND BE OK WITH IT

As has been discussed, we are not perfect. The healthier you get, the more you will be comfortable with your limits. This is a big part of maturity. How many teenagers have you met who know it all? As you grow and develop, you begin to recognize that there are areas where you have strengths and areas where you are not so strong. When you identify the not-so-strong areas, this does not mean that you have to drop everything and make it look like you are an expert in that area, but it does mean you may need to find somebody who is. If you are great at starting a business, you might not be so good at accounting. This does not mean that you need to put your entrepreneurial spirit on ice while you go and get an accounting degree; instead, you may just hire a good accountant. If you get sick, you don't go to medical school, you find a doctor. If you are getting divorced, you don't first go to law school. You hire a lawyer.

It can take some time to figure out that you don't know it all. It can also take some humility. Part of what has made your gatekeeper so strong and effective is the adolescent fantasy that you can do it all by yourself. As you hit a few dead ends and a few walls, you start to learn that perhaps you don't know everything. If you are wise, you can learn this from others. If you are like most of us, you may have to experience the pain for yourself.

As you learn your limits, you can also communicate your limits. As you learn to communicate your limits, you become more healthy. Your boundaries will grow, and your relationships will be enhanced. People will trust you more as you communicate that you have areas where you are not so strong. People will trust your strengths more if you can communicate your weaknesses.

Chapter 12

Bad Happens; Enjoy the Good

If you have been making the investments into your life to not let your seminal event define you, you have begun to find your voice, you have come to grips with life not being fair, and you have asked for help and have actually received it, there is a likelihood that good has shown up in your life. I know it feels weird. Your gatekeeper typically weeds out this good from making through, but historically, when good has snuck (or is it sneaked) its way in, as we discussed earlier, your gatekeeper has only had one response; good must just mean that bad is gonna come, and will likely come with a vengeance to make up for the good kept in. But as you get a chance to slap your gatekeeper, you start to look at good much differently. Instead of fearing or dreading good, you tend to seek ways to enjoy the good. Definitely, bad things will continue to happen because we live in a messed up world. To think that bad has somehow been eradicated like polio is unrealistic. Instead of sitting around and waiting for bad to come, what if you actually enjoyed it when good things make it your way?

LIVE IN THE MOMENT

The more you can stay present in the moment, the more likely you are to enjoy the good. This is a subtle balance. If all we ever do is stay in the moment, with no thought whatsoever of tomorrow, we prepare ourselves for ruin. But if all we ever do is prepare for the future, we never get a chance to enjoy today. And, if we add 'reliving the past' into this mix, it complicates it all the more. So, where is the balance? How do we prepare for the future and live healthily in the moment while successfully learning from the past? Let me offer a few suggestions.

First, let's decatastrophize. I know, that's a big word, and I have trouble saying it. Here's what it means... Let's not assume that anything and everything can totally destroy you. The basic summary here is to replace the "what if" questions with "what is". There is a process to doing this. It starts out by asking yourself;

what you are really worried about. This may take a minute to figure out, but once you do, ask yourself what the worst thing that could happen if this thing you are worried about actually happens. Then, ask yourself...

how likely will that happen? Go ahead and put a number on it. On a scale of 0-100, how likely is that thing to happen? Next, consider...

what is most likely to happen, and get some evidence here to back yourself up. Based on history, what is most likely to happen? Then, think for a moment that...

even if the worst thing does happen, how likely will you be able to sort it in a week, in a month or a year? So circle back and say,...

even if the worst possible thing happens, which is unlikely to happen, there is an "x" percent chance that I will be ok in a week/month/year.

As you work your way through this, what was a catastrophe has lost its power. Now, you are just a little bit more free to live in the moment. You are slowly replacing the 'what if' question with 'what is'...what is real, what is true, what is actually happening instead of what could happen.

A second suggestion to live in the moment involves having a plan or goals. If you know where you are headed and how long it will take you to get there, you can give yourself permission to enjoy the journey. Think of this in terms of finances for a moment. If you have a goal to save $1000, and you determine that you will save $100 a month for 10 months, you set up a budget that allows you to put aside $100 a month while still living your life. When it is time to go out with friends, or buy an article of clothing, if it is a part of the plan, you can make the purchase guilt-free and enjoy the moment because it is part of the plan. Having small, achievable goals that can actually be measured and are part of a larger goal is key here. These are called SMART goals. Goal setting is beyond this scope, but there are tons of resources available to help you dial in healthy, realistic goals for yourself. But if you know where you are going and how long it will take you to get there, you can be freed up to live in the moment.

Third, to fully enjoy living in the moment, determine who is applying the pressure to hurry up. Who is forcing you to push so hard that you cannot enjoy life? Is it self imposed? Is it spouse imposed? Is there a competition you are engaged in? Perhaps your gatekeeper just constantly pushes you to the point that you are never allowed to rest. If you are the only one applying pressure on yourself, why? If it is an external factor, is this person or organization applying pressure for your benefit or theirs? Maybe your job has you on a personal development plan. Is this so you can become a better human or make more money for the company? Is your spouse asking you to gain interpersonal skills to better connect as a couple, or is it so they can beat you up with your past and gaslight you to think that all problems in the relationship are because of you? When you have a chance to figure out who is keeping you from enjoying the moment, you can get an opportunity to use your voice and speak up for yourself.

For a moment, let's talk about how the past can make it difficult to enjoy the present. As it relates to the past, as we have discussed, make sure you are learning from your past and not just simply reliving it. If past experiences are keeping you from enjoying the present, there may be some work to do here. If it is a trauma you have experienced, it may be time to work with a professional who specializes in this area. These interruptions from the past could be in the form of nightmares, or they could just be sounds or smells or objects that trap you in a past experience. This might be more than a gatekeeper issue if you have known triggers. There are really good therapies that can help you overcome past trauma and allow you to live at peace in the present. Nothing will undo what you have gone through, but you can learn to live at peace in the present.

If it is not so much a trauma you are reliving, but more of a mental conversation you are having with yourself, take a moment and remind yourself that you cannot undo the past. It has happened, and there is no way to unhappen it. But you can learn from it and adjust to the present situation. It is possible to choose how much mental energy you give to a situation. With a well-functioning gatekeeper, you can stop the negative thinking and tell yourself it is over and it is time to move on. But this is not where you start.

First, let all five of your senses experience a few somethings in your present. What are three things you see around you? What are three things you hear? What two things can you feel with your sense of touch? What is one thing you smell? One thing you can taste? Then, assess whether or not you are safe. If you are not, get safe. If you are, take a deep breath, and experience a few more somethings from your 5 senses. In the world of therapy, this is called a grounding exercise. Not to ruin it for you, but you just experienced what it is like to live in the moment. As you continue on the journey to enjoy the good, the next step is to start looking for it.

YOU FIND WHAT YOU ARE LOOKING FOR

Have you ever purchased a new (or new-to-you) car and suddenly started seeing the same make, model, or color of your car everywhere? They did not all get purchased at the same time as yours, they have always been on the road, and you were just not looking for it. The same thing happens with finding good. If you are constantly waiting for the next bad thing to happen, you will find it. But, if you begin to look for good to happen, there is a good chance you will find that too! This starts with gratitude.

I know this sounds like a bunch of positive talks, but hang with me for a bit. By seeking out things to be thankful for, you start to look for the good. And if you are new to this journey of finding things to be thankful for, start small. Be thankful you are alive. If you had to pick what clothes to put on today, be thankful you have more than one set of clothes to wear. You can read, or else you have been staring at these strange symbols for a long time, and they're a good number of people in the world who cannot do that. It is good to recite this gratitude to yourself internally, but you may find it more helpful to write it out. Write it out and keep a record of it. Have a gratitude journal. When you find yourself stuck and unable to find things to be grateful for, go reread your journal and get some ideas.

This is not going to happen naturally. You have to intentionally make it happen. You have to purposefully find the good around you, particularly in the early stages of slapping your gatekeeper. At some point along the journey, it will become more natural, but right now, you will have to force yourself to do it. It is going to be awkward, and it will be challenging, but pushing through the difficulty will be worth the effort. Doing this with a friend who is pretty positive makes this a little easier. It may also be necessary to distance yourself from the negative people in your life. If everybody around you is quick to point out the negative or tends to want to give you a negative bent on a situation, your first step to finding positivity might be to set a boundary and hang out less with these people. Nobody is positive all the time. People have bad moments or bad days. But when people around you start having bad weeks and bad months, you may need some support to stay in a relationship with them, especially if you are trying to be more positive.

EXPECT IMPERFECTION

As you start to enjoy the good, you will see that, indeed, good can happen, and is happening all around you. But nobody is perfect. Nobody is good all the time. While this might sound like I am contradicting myself, there is a difference between expecting imperfection and assuming bad will always happen. People will eventually mess up. Situations will eventually not be perfect always. When you can start to expect imperfection, it makes it much easier to deal with it when it comes. It also allows you to enjoy the moments when it just all works out. You may have a really good first date. Don't expect all future dates to be this good; just enjoy this date. If it does not go well the next time, then it's OK. It does not mean this person is a player(or is it playa'). It just meant the first date went well. Now, if all future dates get progressively worse, don't marry this person. Stop going out on dates with him/her.

By recognizing that future moments may not be as good as this moment, you are not dooming yourself to expect bad, but you are giving yourself permission to enjoy the good. We all naturally want consistency. Have you ever gone to a new restaurant and had a great meal, complete with great food, good atmosphere and attentive service, and then went back later and had the opposite experience? Did you go back a third time? While it would be great if life around you was consistently good, your job was consistently stress-free, your friends had an acceptable level of drama, and your car just always worked. Unfortunately, this is just not the case.

Expecting imperfection also means that you will likely need to be prepared for things not to go so well. Practically, this means you might need to find a doctor before you get sick. You may need to have an emergency fund stored up before you have a crisis. You may need to go to the gym before you have a heart attack. It would be a good idea to plan how you will get home before you get drunk. By having a plan in place, you allow yourself the opportunity to enjoy the moment. Even if it does not go perfectly, you can still adapt and overcome. When you live your life too close to the big E, it doesn't take much to run out of gas. Have some reserves, and expect the imperfections.

LAUGH

There are times when it really does not matter how well you planned, how grateful you are, how in the moment you are... Sometimes, things just spectacularly fall apart. On an unprecedented scale, bad can just happen, and then bad calls for reinforcements. When you get to this point, you may need to step back, get to a safe place (if your life is in danger) and just laugh. Laughing at how awesomely awful your situation is, helps you see it from a different perspective. Laughing does not mean that your situation is not bad or is somehow beyond repair, but it gives you a place to reset for a bit and come up with a plan.

Laughter is a powerful reset for your brain. When you can step back and make fun of a situation, you get a chance to calm your threat response system, recognize that you really are OK, and while this awful thing happened, still, it is not over. This is just one stage of the journey. Laughter helps you relax. When you relax, you get a chance to restore energy to the part of your brain that makes good decisions. Then, you can regroup and try again.

Obviously, laughter is not appropriate for every situation. If your life is in danger or someone else's life is in danger, laughter is not the best response. You don't pull up on the scene of a car crash with blood and guts everywhere and start cracking jokes. But after the carnage is addressed, it is not uncommon for first responders to be seen laughing at the conclusion of a tragic scene. It is not that they are cold-hearted or cruel; it is a very natural and healthy way of coping. It helps the brain be able to reset before the next tragedy. This is not to say that a good laugh after a tragic event will somehow remove all traumatic stress, but it is pretty common for people to laugh in the midst of things going horribly wrong.

More than likely, your situation does not meet this threshold of a super tragic event. You could be cooking dinner, and the pot boiled over, the dish in the oven got charred, the potatoes you were going to cook are rotten, and the bread has a fungus on it. And, you figured all of this out as the doorbell is ringing, signaling your guests' arrival. At this point, you have a choice. You can freak out, get supper angry and upset, and just sit on the floor and cry. You can find a corner and hide in it and pretend you are not home, or you can welcome your friends in and have a good laugh together on your way to the restaurant you were not planning to go to. When you are able to take yourself less seriously, you are much more enjoyable to be around. You will also be able to recover much easier and much quicker. Laughter helps you put your situation into perspective.

HOW BAD IS IT?

How bad is your bad? How good is your good? If you are in the middle of a good moment, soak it in. If it is really good, find a way to memorialize it. Take a picture, whether a mental picture or one with your phone. File it away and make sure you can bring it back. See it as a gift and be thankful for it. If it is bad, take a moment to figure out how bad it is. Often, it is not as bad as it may initially appear. When your gatekeeper is working overtime to make you only take in the bad, likely, you will not be able to see anything but the bad in a situation. By understanding how this event fits in the grand scheme of life, you allow yourself a chance to recover. Your life is not over. Yes, there might be a difficult path ahead of you to recovery, but it is not over.

Suppose you find yourself in the middle of an affair. You love your spouse, but you got bored. This other person reminded you of a younger time, and one thing led to another. A few drinks got involved, and you are waking up naked in a hotel room halfway across town to the sound of your phone blowing up with texts and calls from your spouse. It's bad, but it is not over. There is a path out of this. There is a way to recovery that involves honesty and growth. It will also involve a considerable amount of pain. And there is no way to know at this moment what the end might look like. But taking a moment to gain perspective helps you understand that there is a path out of it. It is perspective that helps you choose life in moments like this.

When you lose perspective, you are highly susceptible to suicide. When you don't see a way out of a situation, people who would normally never consider harming themselves make plans to end it all. Perspective helps a person realize there is hope. This is why it is so important that you do not keep plans of hurting yourself to yourself. Talk about it with somebody. Share what is going on in your head with somebody. Talk about your situation before you remove any possibility of acting on your plan to harm yourself.

Grow the muscle of perspective. Start with learning to laugh over the spilled drink instead of cussing it and the world out. Continue to strengthen this when you are running late for an appointment, your tire is flat, and it is starting to rain. The more you are able to grow your ability to laugh your way through situations that are minor, the more you will be able to eventually gain perspective in the larger situations.

VENT

Just get out whatever it is that is bothering you. You know how to change the tire, how to order take out, and how to call a cab and go home, but sometimes you just need to talk it out. We all need a safe place to vent. A vent is just getting out, whatever is bothering you or whatever is really good and happening to you. You don't need a response. You don't need instruction. You just need somebody to listen. The more they offer advice, the less of a vent it is. Here's how you will know you need a vent. As you are telling it, you will just feel better. You will get to the end and feel like a weight is lifted off of your chest.

The person hearing a vent may be unaccustomed to being the recipient of a vent. It is ok to tell this person upfront that you just need to speak and you don't need a response. But, most likely, you are not aware that you don't need a response until after you have shared. It is still ok to tell them you don't need a response, but you just need to talk. And it might not be talk. It might be a scream in the car. It might be an artistic expression that lets you get some emotion out. It might be a physical exercise you do to release some pent-up energy. Whatever it is, as long as it is not harming you or others and gets the frustration out of you, go for it.

Where do you go to vent? Here are a few ideas. Consider writing it down in a journal. Just getting thoughts out of your head and onto paper sometimes is enough to help you organize things and focus on what is really bothering you. If you have healthy friends or family members, go and vent. I visit with people from all over the country who have lived and worked in similar situations as me. We meet up for about an hour or so every few years, and there is safety and confidentiality such that we can exchange vents. None of our problems are solved, but we feel better after the meeting.

Maybe your vent needs to take the form of a prayer. Maybe you should consider yelling it to God. If it is God that you are angry at, tell Him. Tell Him how messed up your situation is and how you expected Him to respond differently. If you don't have a relationship with God or don't have a relationship with healthy enough people who can receive a vent, join a support group. Connecting with a group of strangers who are struggling with the same or similar issue can help you just vent and be heard. This may sound silly, but once you experience its healing power, it will not.

Chapter 13

Fight the Fear

Right about now, this is all sounding good. Logically it makes perfect sense to you. It may not be anything that is particularly new to you. You have likely had similar thoughts throughout the years. But the thought of actually taking the first few steps to slap your gatekeeper is terrifying. Fear is a powerful motivator or a demotivator. As you consider taking steps to change the way you think and interpret the world, let's address fear in a broad sense.

First, maybe you need some additional education. If parts of this seem like they might be making some sense to you, but you are not feeling confident to act, do some more research. Talk with a counselor, read a few more books, and watch some internet videos on the subject from experts. Don't just leap blindly. Get more information. The process of gathering information has a chance to decrease your fear. Let's look at this practically. If you have a fear of flying, it might be good to do some research and see how planes actually work. Also, investigating the odds of a crash, understanding the safety equipment on board, the checks and balances of aircraft maintenance, air traffic control, and how pilots actually get trained can go a long way to reducing your fears.

Second, get some perspective. Ask somebody else what they think. If you ask a few people and they too are scared for you, listen to the fear. But likely, your fear has grown beyond the bounds of healthy. Your fears may be over-compensating and overactive. If you talk to friends, healthy friends, about making some lifestyle changes and they are encouraging and supportive, it can help lower your fear. If you don't have healthy friends, hire them. Go see a counselor or a life coach, and get their perspective. Share this with your support group and see if they look at you like you have a third eye. If you have reason to be afraid, listen to the fear. But if healthy people in your life tell you otherwise, take the first steps.

Third, you don't have to jump in headfirst. You can take a few steps and evaluate. Making major changes, the types of changes that involve going against an internal voice that has been telling you what to do and what not to do for years, is really hard. Don't expect it to just happen like flipping a switch. Take a few steps, make a few changes, and then evaluate. If you like the direction you are going, keep walking. If you don't, stop. Don't fall into the trap of having to be perfect. You will not go through these changes perfectly. Nobody does. Perfection can be a horrible enemy to fight. Making perfection the standard is a great way to always be discouraged. Give yourself space to mess up. It will be a little messy, and that is perfectly OK!

Fourth, get a healthy insight on the difference between hard and bad. Just because the steps to a healthier you are hard does not make them bad. If you are trying to lose weight, staying on a diet is hard, but seeing the scale return a lower number is good. But if you stick with it for a few weeks and the diet sucks, and you are gaining weight, go talk to a doctor or a nutritionist and get a new plan. Remember, it is your responsibility to change yourself. When you have a plan, you are taking responsibility. It is ok that plans change. Changing plans means you have movement. Movement means you are not stuck.

Invest in your present, plant the seeds of good relationships, make changes to become a better you, accomplish the goals you want for yourself, and slap your gatekeeper!

PART 4

Change the Gatekeeper

If you have made it this far and you have taken steps to begin the process of slapping your gatekeeper, let me just say how excited and happy I am for you. This is not easy work, and if you are putting into practice what we have already discussed, I can only imagine how difficult this has been for you. Take a moment and reflect on how different life is starting to look. Different in a good way! Part Three is about helping you maintain your progress. While you may have turned down the volume on the unhealthy voice through a series of slaps, I want to help you grow a healthy gatekeeper. I wish I could tell you that the old gatekeeper has been vanquished, but I have learned that he tends to go dormant for some time, and if you don't take healthy steps to keep him at bay, he will resurface. As you begin to transition to a new way of living, there will likely need to be a myth you will need to bust. You cannot undo what was done. You cannot get a redo. There is no control(or command)-Z button in life. Life is not going back to the way it was. You don't get a second childhood, can't start over with a new family, and you will not be able to put the genie back into the bottle. Part of what keeps the gatekeeper at bay is learning to accept the reality of the world you live in, and that world is different from the world that exists (or existed) in your hopes and dreams.

I don't mean this to sound harsh or uncaring, but I have walked this journey with people who hold on to an unattainable hope of having their innocence restored. For the addict, you will always know what that first high felt like. There will never be a time when that will not be a temptation for you at some level. If you can accept that, you can then take the steps below to be healthy and sober. If you have experienced trauma, you will never go back to a way of living that is not influenced by trauma. If you can accept that your life is now trauma-influenced, you can establish healthy plans, so your life is not dominated by trauma. Once you experience a panic attack, you cannot un-experience it. It happened, and it sucked, but you can gain healthy tools to make it, so your life does not have to be controlled by panic.

So let's talk about these healthy steps. These steps are not some magical formula, they are not easy, and they are not exact. As you see them unfold, I hope you will begin to see that these are a part of overall healthy life. Healthy living may be new to you, so permit yourself to go slow. As you gain traction towards healthy living, you also start to grow a healthy gatekeeper.

Chapter 14

Routines

That's right! It is the four-letter R-word. Routines! Routines can get a bad wrap as being boring and restrictive, but in reality, they are just the opposite. When you have healthy routines in your life, you have the resources you need to thrive healthily. Routines are like the small building blocks that make up a much larger structure. When you begin to set healthy goals for yourself, your routines help you to accomplish those goals. Like any good thing, routines can go too far. It is not healthy when your routines control you; instead of you controlling your routines. If anxiety is a part of your past, your old gatekeeper can resurface and tell you that it is the routine keeping you healthy and not you, and you better keep doing that routine or else. Remember, you are to be in control of your routines. When routines start to control you, they can become compulsions. And it can get really easy to obsess over these compulsions. I mention this as a point of caution because if this fear of creating compulsions is a part of what is keeping you from creating healthy routines, we still have some gatekeeper slapping to do. A healthy you makes healthy choices, and a healthy you will be healthily in control of your routines because your routines are helping you accomplish your goals.

On the other end of the spectrum, a different perversion of a healthy routine is a rut. A routine brings life and growth, and a rut keeps you stuck. Here are a few examples to consider. Exercise is a healthy routine, and sitting on the couch and watching your favorite streaming platform is a rut. Meal prepping a certain day each week is a healthy routine. Ordering fast food to be delivered to you because you forgot to buy groceries is a rut. Having regular meetings with friends to socialize and support each other is a healthy routine, while isolating is a rut.

Healthy routines help you grow. Unhealthy routines (whether compulsions or ruts) trap you and keep you stuck. If you are feeling trapped or stuck, you can change your routine! Remember, you own the routine. You can keep it, chunk it, expand it, or restrict it. If you feel like you can't make those types of changes, go talk to somebody and get some help.

In the early stages, routines can be small. Perhaps routinely taking a shower is a good place to start. It could also be something as simple as taking your medications or making your bed, which involves getting out of it and not returning to your bed. As you are able to successfully complete small routines, consider what routines you might need to add to accomplish the larger goal of thriving. Taking small steps towards larger goals is really healthy. Admiral William H. McRaven wrote a book titled "Make Your Bed: Little Things That Can Change Your Life...And Maybe the World," in which he goes into detail about the importance of just doing one small thing each day, and doing that thing right, just like making your bed.

Healthy routines are also great ways to monitor your progress. Particularly if you have a mental illness, having healthy routines gives you a way to measure your mental health, as it can be difficult to track depression or anxiety. If you are able to accomplish your healthy routines, it is a good indicator of your overall functionality. If you are not able to complete your healthy routines, it is a good warning sign it might be time to talk with a counselor, adjust medications with your doctor, or maybe a good time just to go and vent to a friend.

There will be days when you may not feel like doing anything. If you have established healthy routines and trust that those routines are healthy because a healthy you created them, you can trust the routine when you can't trust your motivation or energy levels. By completing the routines, you can keep depression or anxiety well managed. This is not to say that healthy routines will magically cure mental illness, but by knowing to engage in healthy activities even when you don't feel like it, those healthy routines can keep you healthy. For example, you may not feel like taking your medication. If you have established a morning routine that involves taking your medication and getting dressed, it can keep you from forgetting and isolating yourself in your bed. If you were to just stay in bed and forget meds for a day or two, before long, you have slipped back into a depressive episode. But with the routine, you can keep it at bay.

Chapter 15

Relationships

Previously, we discussed the importance of establishing relationships, particularly with the help of professionals. Establishing and maintaining those relationships is still important, but not exactly what we are talking about here. Think of those relationships as reactionary. You needed them to deal with a problem you already had. To keep the gatekeeper slapped and to grow a healthy gatekeeper, you need relationships to help you with problems before you have them. These are more like proactive relationships.

Let's see if I can illustrate this with a personal example. I have GI issues (let's just keep it at that, and I will spare you the unpleasant details), and I moved to another state. The stress of that move activated the GI issues. When I moved to the new state, it meant that I needed to change doctors. Had I been healthier and followed these principles better, I would have been proactive about setting up care with a doctor in advance. However, what I wound up doing was waiting until I got there, got new insurance, and then just called somebody on the list and tried to get an appointment.

I moved in June, and the first appointment was in November. From June to November, I went to the hospital 3 times, lost about 30 pounds, and was generally sick way more than I needed to be. If you have relationships before you need them, it makes it much easier to get help when you need it, the right kind of help that you actually need.

Proactive relationships allow you to look ahead and anticipate the needs you will eventually have. These can be professional relationships, but they are also work-related and personal relationships. From a health perspective, it is a good idea to have a primary care physician. Go and establish with somebody when you are not sick. Figure out which hospital you would choose to go to in your area before you are in the back of an ambulance. Make sure your doctor has privileges at that hospital. If you are moving to a new area, work now to establish care in a new place. Go and visit your current providers, fill out releases, get an adequate supply of medication, and be prepared. Your vehicle will eventually break down. Ask around to see who would be a good mechanic.

From a work-related standpoint, this can be called networking. Take a chance to do a meet-and-greet with a few professionals in your area. This might also mean being a part of a local business club. You may also want to read the books that the type of people you want to work for have written. If you are looking to get hired for a certain job, restructure your social media profiles to connect with the people who are connected with the people who want to hire you. Then, make a point to go meet them. This could be a conference they are speaking at, send an email and ask for a coffee meeting purposely to just ask them about themselves. Don't go stalk these people like a creeper, but take a chance and ask. Everybody had to start somewhere, and most enjoyed the opportunity to help others. Having a good professional network is a valuable way to help you get employment, maintain employment, and at some point in the future, gives you a good source of people to reach out to and hire when you get to be the boss!

From a personal standpoint, resist the urge to be in the my-4-no-more crowd. Inevitably, you will have a few really close friends, but keep making connections. Find friends who are different from you, who have strengths you do not have. Meet people and have conversations with people who disagree with you. Most importantly, get to know healthy people. People who have definable and observable successes in their life. If you are a parent, find people who have raised healthy kids. Talk to them about their challenges and success as a parent. See what they did to be successful and do that. They have likely figured out a thing or two along the way. If you are married, find an older married couple who looks like they still enjoy being together and ask for a double date. These healthy friendships may be from unconventional sources. They may not be your same age, ethnicity, or culture. And that is awesome! Meeting people different from you grows and challenges you. The people who are most similar to you are likely messed up. Part of growing in health is going to be establishing a healthier way to live, and who better to be that guide than people who are living healthily.

If you decide to take a chance and reach out to somebody who appears to be successful, here are a few tips to let you know if you have found the right person. If they get the drift that you are looking for advice and they proceed to tell you what an expert they are and that they are perfect in every way... these are not your people. If they look a little shocked and tell you that you likely have the wrong person because they have made mistakes after mistake and just kept going...there is a good chance these are your people. You are not looking for perfect people here, but authentic people.

Healthy friends do not grow on trees. It would be nice if they did. You could just go outside, pick four or five, fill up your basket, and bam, healthy support network. While they do not grow on trees, I believe that you can plant the seeds of a healthy relationship and eventually reap the harvest of healthy relationships. It takes time. Don't wait until you need healthy friends to try and find healthy friends. You do this proactively. If you focus on being the type of friend that a healthy friend would want to have, you will find this process much easier. Be friendly, have good boundaries, don't be needy, and contribute to the relationship. Your unhealthy gatekeeper might be telling you that you have nothing to give, but if you have gone down the road this far, you have figured a few things out about yourself as well as life. This is valuable information to share. Healthy people will want to hear this.

Chapter 16

Physical Resources

As you are growing your healthy gatekeeper, you will need resources to help this gatekeeper grow. Just like there were unhealthy nutrients that allowed your unhealthy gatekeeper to take over, there are healthy nutrients that will allow your gatekeeper to grow healthy. I want to break these down into three categories; physical resources, emotional resources, and spiritual resources.

Physical Resources

Your physical body needs to be healthy for your gatekeeper to be healthy. This does not mean that unless you are the picture-perfect example of health, you cannot have a healthy gatekeeper, but it does mean you need to take care of yourself. We know from numerous studies that those who have had adverse childhood experiences are more likely to develop physical symptoms later in life. Everything from autoimmune disorders to heart conditions, you name it. The extra stress hormones that your brain has sent coursing through your system to keep you alive will, at some point, create issues. So here are a few things to consider. As you read this, remember to start small. The goal is not to accomplish all of this in one weekend but to make subtle changes so that you can ultimately change your tastes and exceptions for yourself. There is no particular order to these, and some may be harder for you than it would be for others.

FOOD

Pay attention to what you eat. What fuel you give your body determines how well it can perform. If your food groups are pan-fried, deep-fried and chicken fried, it might be time for a change. I am not saying you have to eat kale-wrapped tofu, but pay attention to what you are eating. We have referenced this earlier in the section on routines, but just eating at regular intervals is a really powerful resource. As you begin to eat regularly, see if there is one thing you can substitute in your diet that could be healthy; drink water instead of soda, order broccoli instead of fries, and try grilled instead of fried. I have learned from personal experience that trying to change everything overnight is likely unlikely to yield lasting results. Restrictive diets might help you with a short-term goal, but I have seen too many people go on a restrictive diet and lose the weight they set out to, only to gain it back because their overall lifestyle did not change. If you have no idea where to start, a consultation with a nutritionist might be a professional relationship you need to add to your toolbox.

MOVEMENT

The second area of health where your physical body can benefit is simply moving your body. Notice I am not using the "E" word(exercise). Just move your body. If joining a gym is helpful, then go all out and exercise. Become a social media influencer if that is your jam. But if not, start small. Go for a walk, ride a bike, find a physical activity you can healthily enjoy, and do it. Play racket ball, golf, frisbee golf, mow your grass, go for a hike, go for a swim, kayak... the options are numerous. As an added bonus, many of these activities can easily involve people. Are you starting to catch a theme here? This is awesome if you can engage in a group activity like martial arts, dance, theater, or yoga. There is a significant amount of help that can be achieved for trauma survivors who learn how to control their bodies through these types of activities. This is not saying that you have to spend a lot of money doing this, just move your body. Movement is healthy for you physically as well as mentally. For some, physical fitness is way more than something that is just physical. It is possible there are some deep-seated pains that are associated with how you see yourself physically. As you get healthy internally, don't neglect your physical body. It needs to grow too.

SLEEP

Rounding out the big three in the physical body category is sleep. No joke, every intake I do with a new patient involves these three areas. I ask them how they are eating, what type of movement is in their life, and how well they are sleeping. When your sleep is significantly and consistently off, your opportunity to live in the land of the healthy is limited. There are a number of factors that can interrupt sleep, from medications you are taking, your diet, and your overall mental health, to just environmental factors like noise, temperature, and other people. While there may be parts of this you cannot control, let's talk about what you can control. Let's assume you work a schedule where you sleep at night and work during the day. If that is the opposite for you, the principles below apply, but the times will be different.

Healthy sleep starts as soon as you get up in the morning. Wake up at roughly the same time (remember routines?). As you begin to wake up at the same time, you are able to start conditioning your body as to when it is sleep time and when it is wake time. When you wake up, get out of bed. Don't stay in bed and read, work on homework, pay bills, and watch TV. If you stay in bed, your brain starts to think this is the place where you need to be alert and active. Then at night time, you get in bed, and your brain goes, "ok, let's get to work!" Which is the opposite of what you want your brain doing at night. Also, get bright. Open up the windows and let some light in. If you don't have windows, turn on some really bright lights. If you don't have bright lights, perhaps a trip to the store is in your future. By having light in your face, you give yourself the opportunity to remind your brain that it is time to wake up. And while you are up, eat something. Food helps start multiple internal systems.

By mid-day, don't let tiredness ruin your plans. Now, if you can't stay awake, don't doze and dive, but stick to your plan. If you were gonna go hang out with friends, but you are tired, then be tired with your friends. Resist the urge to nap. If you are gonna nap, limit it to less than 30 minutes, and no naps after 4 pm. Also, finish any caffeine by this time as well. By the time you get into early evening, it is a good idea to limit or avoid alcohol. While alcohol may help slow your system down, and many believe it is necessary to get ready for sleep (assuming that it is not negatively interacting with your medications), it will not help you achieve the deep sleep you ultimately need.

By bedtime, have really good bedtime routines. An hour before bed, turn off screens...TVs, phones, tablets, computers, etc. In the same way that lights in the morning helps wake you up, lights in the evening keep you awake. Start to dim your lights about an hour before bed. Turn on calm music. If your thoughts race, do a data dump. Write down all that you think so you can begin to train yourself on how to shut your brain down. Do the same things every night before bed; this might be a bath/shower, brushing teeth, changing clothes, journaling, etc. By being consistent, you are training your body and brain how to shut down and prepare for sleep.

When you get in bed, focus on relaxing your body. Start with your toes, squeeze them, take a deep breath, and as you exhale, focus on relaxing your toes. Move up to your calves, thighs, butt, stomach, chest, arms and face. Go from toes to head, then head to toes. As you are focusing your mind on what your body is feeling, you are training your brain to shut down other thoughts and stay on one thing. If, after about 20-30 minutes, you are still finding yourself wide awake, get out of bed. Go and do something calm and boring. Find a really boring book, a jigsaw puzzle, play solitaire or do anything that does not involve a lot of light or a screen. When you catch yourself getting tired, go back to bed and try it again.

MEDICAL

If you go for more than three nights without being able to sleep healthily, you will want to take advantage of the next resource associated with physical health; seeing a doctor. In general, you need to have relationships with the medical community. This is a tremendous resource for a healthy you. Establish care with somebody. If you don't have insurance, consider talking with an independent insurance agent and find a cheap plan. If you do, you don't have an excuse. Most plans cover physicals and preventative care almost completely. It is WAY cheaper for an insurance company to keep you healthy than to pay to get you repaired after years of neglect. Healthy people go to doctors regularly. Healthy people get blood work done and monitor internal systems. If something is off, they address it proactively. If you want to meet a hot fireman in uniform, bring cookies to the fire station, don't use a heart attack as an ice breaker!

MONEY

Unrelated to your body, let's talk finances for a moment. Finances are a really healthy resource you will need to have. Let me clue you into a really complicated principle related to finances. In order to have health in this area, you have to spend less than you make. That's it. People pay a lot of money for that, and I just dropped that truth bomb on you like it was nothing. You need to spend less than you make. Or let me say it another way, you have to make more than you spend. If this is a foreign concept to you, just start writing down everything that you spend money on for a month. At the end of the month, look at what you wrote down. If you spent less than what you made and like how you spent money, that is your budget. If you have debt, establish a plan to pay off your debt. I know you hear all kinds of stories of how really wealthy people use debt as a tool to build more wealth. But here's the catch. THAT AIN'T YOU! Having an emergency fund, being debt-free, and living on a budget is an overwhelmingly powerful resource for your health. Think about how much stress and anxiety comes into your life when your tires go flat, your AC starts blowing hot air, you have a medical emergency, or anything unplanned comes your way that is going to cost money? What about when the planned happens, like Christmas or birthdays, and they come every year, and they cost money too! If you have a plan, you have peace where you once had anxiety. Take some time to go to a financial class, read some books, and hire a financial advisor. Your finances are a tremendous resource that will help you accomplish your goals of growing a healthy gatekeeper.

Chapter 17

Emotional Resources

Your mind needs health just the same way your body does. The resources we discussed as being healthy for your body are also a really good foundation for you to have a healthy mind. In addition to these, let's see if we can flesh out a few other areas where you might be able to find healthy ways to process your emotions.

COMMUNICATE VS. EXPERIENCE

You have emotions; you do. And you need to feel them. Suppressing them is not doing anybody any good. Your body produces your emotions based on how you interpret what you see, what you hear, what you touch, what you smell, and what you taste. Once your brain takes in something from your five senses, you interpret that based on your beliefs, experiences, and expectations, and then you get emotions. Emotions are pretty logical. How you interpret things will determine your emotions.

For example, if I came home to my wife and found her sitting on the couch, eating cheese puffs and watching reruns, I might interpret that my wife is just plain lazy. If I do not value laziness and she asks me to take out the trash, I might think that my wife is not doing her fair share around the house, and I might think that she is taking advantage of me, and I might feel angry and hurt. However, if my wife has been really sick and in bed for the past three days, the fact that she is sitting up on the couch and eating something, I might interpret that as a sign that she is getting better, and the fact that there is something in the trash means she put something in it, and I might start to get really happy that she is recovering. It is the same set of data that is coming, but my interpretations of that data determine my emotions.

Why the long explanation of emotions? Emotions are great motivators, but they are terrible navigators. Feel your emotions, find ways to process your emotions, but don't let your emotions control you. Let's go back to my cheese puff eating wife. If I am really angry at her, and I just go off, start yelling and throwing things, I will likely not solve my problem. But instead, if I take a moment, ideally on my way to the trash can, and feel my emotions, then process where they are coming from, I can then set a date and time to discuss my concerns with my wife. Here is the key. Be prepared because this one is huge. When you are working healthily with emotions, you can communicate your emotions to someone rather than just simply expressing your emotions. You can tell somebody you are sad without having to cry. You can tell somebody you are angry without having to cuss. You can tell somebody you love them without having sex with them.

EMOTIONAL TRAPS

Sometimes, it can get overwhelming to experience some emotions. Perhaps they are connected to some really old wounds. Maybe some emotions have to lead to a shutdown and a really dark path. Remember, that was the old you. Healthy you have different tools and no longer have to avoid those emotions. If you are avoiding certain topics or emotions, you have some work to do. This is not bad. It is really healthy that you can identify this, but you do have some work to do. Let me encourage you while you are here to avoid a few emotional traps.

If you are doing something to numb your pain, this is not going to help you form a healthy gatekeeper. This could be a substance, an activity, a person, or anything that you might use to distract and numb yourself. These can be really unhealthy like drugs, alcohol, pornography, sex, overeating, over-shopping, gambling, etc. But, these can also be things that the rest of the world might see as healthy, but for you, they are just distractions you are using to avoid dealing with the real issue. Maybe you are volunteering more and more at church to avoid a conflict at home, and perhaps you won't leave the gym because exercise has stopped being something healthy but has become a compulsion. Maybe your attempts to save money have led you down the rabbit hole of couponing, and you are buying things you don't need just to save money!

Whatever the distraction, a healthy gatekeeper will help you to see that these are not helping you grow; they are keeping you stuck. I know what I am about to discuss is going to ask you to be really vulnerable, but consider letting a friend in on what is really going on. If not a friend, talk with a therapist. If you are getting snared in emotional traps, take some time to figure out what is at the root and process that emotion. When you do, you will find freedom.

Chapter 18

Spiritual Resources

Before you think about tossing this book and skipping this last section, let me tell you this is not a guilt-ridden plea for religion. This is about you connecting to a meaning and purpose for your life. For some, that might involve a house of worship, and for others, maybe not. As you journey towards spiritual health, there are a few questions that you will need to consider. And note that I said you need to consider this. There are plenty of people who will try and convince you that their way of interpreting this is the right way. I have found that if somebody can convince me, somebody else can un-convince me. This is why it is good to go on this journey and figure these things out personally. Here are the questions; why am I here, why do I suffer, and what happens when I am gone. Let's look at them one at a time and see why their answers are important to growing a healthy gatekeeper.

WHY AM I HERE?

It is highly possible that you have asked this question to your old gatekeeper, and he has given you a pretty sorry answer. An unhealthy gatekeeper will try to convince you that you are a mistake, an accident, and nobody wants you. But a healthy gatekeeper knows different. When you have a healthy spiritual connection, you can begin to understand that there is a reason you are here. Maybe you were an accidental surprise, but you are here. Perhaps your parents put you up for adoption, and you have bounced in and out of foster homes ever since. I don't want to give you a one-liner to make all of that better, but having healthy spiritual resources help you make sense of it.

As you take time to understand why you are here, you start to understand that there is some sort of meaning and purpose to your life. This is the foundation for how you begin to develop value as a person. This might sound like an out-there concept, but having value as a person is a huge foundation for growing a healthy gatekeeper. Understanding your value and why you have value is not a simple task. For far too many people, their value is unhealthily based on performance. In other words, I am only as good as what I produce. I am only as good as the money I make, the races I win, the cars I drive, the vacations I take, the lives I save... the list could go on and on, but here's the point. These things are not necessarily bad things, but these things cannot be what brings you value. You do these things because you are valuable. When you know your worth, you can produce from a place of strength, not produce to become. You make money because you are smart and creative and have a healthy system for evaluating risks. You win races because you are a good athlete and you enjoy running. Are you starting to see the difference?

As this relates to a healthy gatekeeper, when you know why you are here and what brings you value and worth, when an investment goes bad, you are still valuable. You are not less-than when you lose a race. You are still you. And a healthy gatekeeper will remind you of this. If you are valuable and you know it, it feels pretty good to be you, win or lose. (I know it feels better to win, but losing does not rob you of your value and worth.)

So how do you figure this out? How do you know what your value and worth is? I wish I could just give you the answer. Have you scanned the QR code and poof...there it is. However, it is very good to take some time and struggle with this question. You may not have delved deep enough if you get a quick and easy answer. For some, this answer is found in a relationship with God, who has fearfully and wonderfully knit you together in your mother's womb. For others, it is all about science and biology. Whatever end of the spectrum you are on, it is important that you know what your value and worth is, and this is most likely going to be found when you are able to fully and confidently answer the question of why you are here.

WHY DO I SUFFER?

In the 5th century BC, a Nepalese prince named Siddhartha Gautama walked out of his lavish palace and was struck by the suffering of those who were less fortunate than he was. He set out to understand this. Ultimately, this led him to enlightenment, and today some 470 million Buddhists follow his teachings. The answer to the question of why people suffer is foundational to every major world religion. For Christianity, suffering is about refinement. As I suffer, the parts of me that are sinful or undesirable are transformed. For those who follow multiple gods, suffering means that a deity is somehow upset with you, and you need to figure out how to properly appease the correct god so as to alleviate this suffering.

As you develop healthy spiritual resources, you will want to get an answer to this question because one thing is pretty much for sure... you will experience suffering. If you know the purpose of your suffering, it makes it a lot easier to endure. Viktor Frankl wrote a book in 1946 called Man's Search for Meaning. In it, he described in pretty horrifying detail his time in a Nazi concentration camp. What he began to notice was how seemingly healthy people would not last very long, and some really unhealthy people would just continue to survive despite all odds. He determined that if you have a reason or purpose for why you are enduring hardships, you can endure much more and much longer than those who do not have a reason or purpose. When you lack meaning or purpose, you don't tend to survive all that well.

While you may not have a challenge as horrifying as a concentration camp in your near future, you do have suffering that you have survived, and you will endure suffering. In the 2012 action movie Act of Valor, the movie depicts a rescue of a covert operative who was captured and tortured by a terrorist. After executing an adrenaline-packed rescue and an action-packed escape, they board their rescue boat, and one of the members of the rescue team pulls a cell phone that belonged to the terrorist out of his pocket and shows it to the recently rescued but brutally tortured operative, and says, "It wasn't for nothing." This means we got information and intelligence to help us get closer to catching the guy. Yes, you suffered, but you suffered for a purpose.

As you endure suffering in your life, knowing why, or having a reasonable conclusion, is fuel for a healthy gate-keeper to help you continue and not give up. This is not to say that you will never get discouraged or that you will never get frustrated, but with healthy spiritual resources, you can at least make sense of it. Even if you understand that there is no reason or purpose for suffering, at least you have thought it through.

WHAT HAPPENS WHEN I AM GONE?

If you know why you are here and why you suffer, the next big question to consider as you grow your spiritual resources is to give some thought to what happens when you are no longer here. I don't mean to rain on any parades, but at some point, we all come to an end. Then what? Is that it, and we are just gone? Is there a heaven or a hell? Do we come back as something else? Is there a spiritual world where we go to guide our descendants? Do we get our own planet in the afterlife? These are the questions that you answer with a healthy spiritual resource. Answers to this question go a long way to providing you with reason and purpose in this life. When you know what the end goal is, it makes it much easier to run the race.

Could you imagine running a race, and at the start of that race, nobody told you how long the race was going to be? Do you run as fast as you can because this is a 100-yard dash and it is necessary to use up all your energy as quickly as you can? Or is this some 100-mile extreme distance race, and if you try and sprint the whole thing, you will find out sooner than later what exactly happens when you are gone? Knowing what happens when you are no longer here allows you to better prepare for life. If all of your treasures are to be laid up in heaven, then you live your life differently on earth. If man is the measure, and this life is all you have, you will live it much differently. If you are to navigate the middle way on your journey to nirvana, this will influence how you live out your day to day life.

Ultimately, this leads you to a journey of faith, as there is really no way of knowing what will happen after you are gone until you are gone and experience it for yourself. But with strong spiritual resources, you will be able to grow your faith, and faith is a good thing. Faith and hope tend to hang out together. If we can help you grow one, you will likely get the other. We have discussed how easy it is to lose hope and how unhealthy gatekeepers have kept hope away for proposed protection. But as you grow this spiritual resource, you get a chance to really investigate what faith is, and that journey into faith can help you grow hope.

If all of this discussion on spirituality is freaking you out a bit, don't feel like you need to figure it all out now. This is a lifelong journey. It is ok. In fact, it is preferred to take it slow. Ask questions. As you meet healthy people, see what role their spirituality plays in their life and how it contributes to their health. If you start to hear some common themes, investigate a little further. If asking those questions just makes you more confused, then keep asking questions. Confusion is not always a bad thing. It means you are thinking for yourself and that your unhealthy gate-keeper is not in charge.

Chapter 19

Final Thoughts

It is my hope and prayer that this work helps you on your journey to health. I hope that you have found hope while reading, and that you are able to find help along the way. As I have walked with so many who are on this road to healing, I am learning how challenging this journey can be, and you have my greatest respect for taking a stand and making some changes in your life. Please do not get discouraged if the progress is slow. Allow yourself to focus on small victories, and take time to celebrate your success.

If you have finished this work because a loved one is going through an intense battle with mental health and you are trying to understand them better, let me offer one final piece of advice. Nobody wants to feel like a project. Please do not set out to "fix" anybody in your life. My hope is that this work has helped you better understand your loved one so you can be a better friend. When I ask those on this journey what they want their friends to know about their mental illness, they frequently tell me that they just want somebody to listen to them and understand them. If you have taken the time to read this, good for you. You are headed in a really good direction to just ask questions from your friend and take time to listen. Just because I have detailed what some go through, it does not mean this is a narrative for all who are struggling with mental health. I encourage you to lead with empathy. Take time to understand what your loved one is going through, and be their friend. Listen, love and support them, help them call out their negative gatekeeper, and help model what a healthy gatekeeper sounds or looks like.

About the Author

Douglas Hodges has been married since 2003, and is the father of two boys. He is a licensed as a mental health counselor in the state of Florida, serving in a leadership position at the agency where he works while managing a caseload of individuals, couples, and groups. On weekends, you may find Douglas behind the audio console volunteering at his church, at a theme park with his family, or paddling down a random river.